Eat & Explore

North Carolina

Favorite Recipes, Celebrations
& Travel Destinations

Christy Campbell

Great American Publishers

www.GreatAmericanPublishers.com

TOLL-FREE 1-888-854-5954

Great American Publishers

P. O. Box 1305 • Kosciusko, MS 39090

TOLL-FREE **1-888-854-5954 • www.GreatAmericanPublishers.com**

ISBN 978-1-934817-18-6

First Edition
10 9 8 7 6 5 4 3 2 1

by Christy Campbell

Front cover photo: © iStock/Dave Allen
Cover illustration: Mark P. Anderson, Big Whiskey Design Studio
Back cover photo: courtesy of Shelton Vineyards
Back cover food image: Spicy Peanut Soup by Jerry Deutsch

Chapter opening photos: Appetizers & Beverages © Smokingdrum/istockphoto.com
Bread & Breakfast © Tannjuska/thinkstock.com • Soups & Salads © funwithfood/istockphoto.com
Vegetables & Other Side Dishes © Diana Didyk/istockphoto.com
Meat & Seafood © Ezhicheg/istockphoto.com
Desserts & Other Sweets © Edward ONeil Photography/istockphoto.com
Index © Roberto Zocchi/istock.com

Every effort has been made to ensure the accuracy of the information provided in this book.
However, dates, times, and locations are subject to change.
Please call or visit websites for up-to-date information before traveling.

To purchase books in quantity for corporate use, incentives, or fundraising,
please call Great American Publishers at 1-888-854-5954.

Eat & Explore
North Carolina

Contents

Introduction

While pondering the five states we've explored in the EAT & EXPLORE STATE COOKBOOK SERIES, I find myself asking "how has this journey led me here?" I find myself back on the Eastern side of this great country, and I am filled with awe and gratitude at the amazing opportunity I've been given to learn more about the nooks and crannies of America. So here I am, looking over the pages of what will be the sixth book in the EAT & EXPLORE STATE COOKBOOK SERIES, and I am wondering, as I have done with other states, what is it like to live in North Carolina? There are mountains and beaches, hip communities and cultural meccas, historic landmarks and sacred grounds. . . . North Carolina seems to have it all. Growing up, one of my favorite family vacations led us to the Tar Heel State. I remember the exhilaration of white water rafting down the Nantahala, and the quaint, charming towns that seemed to jump out of the pages of novels written about the South. This is where I found the answer to my question. This journey has led me here because I am being guided along a path of both remembrance and new experiences. As always, along this path a picture is formed in my mind. Today this picture is of North Carolina, of living daily life with clear mountain streams. I know towns ripe with history and beautiful beaches where horses run free. There is now another piece of the patchwork quilt completed, taking me another step along the trail of discovery that leads to North Carolina.

The first attempt at colonization in North America was made in North Carolina, and I imagine this is because it is a land of beauty and resources. Explorers discovering the Outer Banks would have been in awe of the breathtaking views of beaches, mountains, forests and plains. As this bountiful area was settled by early explorers, communities began to form that would one day become creative centers for art and music. Today, North Carolina boasts cities such as Asheville, a city that is known as being home to artists, musicians, and visionaries. It is also a leading cotton producer, with rolling snow-white fields stretching far and wide. North Carolina is a destination for those seeking to soak up the sun and sand on relaxing beaches. The treasures found in North Carolina are many, and this is evident in the thousands of travelers that visit the Tar Heel State, year after year.

As an image of North Carolina has formed in my mind, visions of gatherings with family and friends have emerged. I envision bright kitchens with bowls of fresh vegetables, the scent of hand-made soaps subtly filling the room. I imagined succulent cakes baked to perfection, and children running through large yards flying kites and playing ball. *Carmel's Goat Cheese-Tomato Bisque, Ginger-Glazed Bison Meatballs, Blueberry French-Toast Muffins,* and *Bourbon-Glazed Rib-Eyes* are local favorites welcome at every meal. The deliciousness continues with *Braised Lamb Shanks, Havarti Chive Mashed*

Potatoes, Out-On-A-Limb Red Apple Salsa and *Graham County Bread*. When it's time to satisfy a sweet tooth, *Strawberry-Almond Cream Tart, Grammy's Delicious Molasses Cookies, Blueberry Sonker* and *Honey Pecan Pie* will do the trick!

With each passing year, Great American Publishers evolves and grows. Every day brings surprises and accomplishments, and each new cookbook we produce is a tribute to the hard work and dedication of our terrific staff. Brooke Craig keeps her eye on every aspect of what we do, guiding the business down a path of success. Author and sales manager Krista Griffin brightens each day with her positive attitude and funny stories. Author Anita Musgrove is hard at work making our mark in the world with the STATE BACK ROAD RESTAURANTS COOKBOOK SERIES. Diane Rothery and Pam Edwards are the glue that holds it all together, and each of these fine ladies get me out of scrapes on a weekly basis! Without these women I would not be able to get it all done, and I am grateful for each of them, more than they know.

I have to give a special and sincere acknowledgement to the other Christy Campbell at Great American Publishers. Brooke Craig made a joke once with regards to the EAT & EXPLORE STATE COOKBOOK SERIES, saying we just needed another Christy Campbell. Well, low and behold we found one, but in no way is she just someone who shares a name with me. Christy Kent Campbell was the driving force behind the first half of this book's creation. It is through her love of North Carolina, her hard work and willingness to reach for higher heights, and the unique gracefulness she possesses that this book is a reality. Thank you, Christy, for all the qualities you bring to the table, for each are valuable assets that our team is blessed to have.

Sheila and Roger Simmons are mainstays now in my life. We don't always agree on the process, but we do always agree on the vision. It is this long-term sight and sincere friendship that binds us together. Cyndi Clark's creative gifts are indeed works of art. I cannot imagine doing any of this without this team of dedicated individuals.

My sons, Michael and Preston, are now 11 and 10. I watch them grow, and I love the personalities that have emerged as they enter into the next phase of their lives. My husband Michael is infinitely patient with the time I spend creating these cookbooks, and I hope he knows it does not go without notice.

The wonderful state of North Carolina is the sixth state explored in the EAT & EXPLORE STATE COOKBOOK SERIES. The journey to this state has let me know that I am on a path that winds and turns, but does not end. And for that I am forever grateful. Thank you for taking this stop with me to . . . North Carolina.

Chris Campbell

Appetizers & Beverages

Southwest Banana Pepper Dip

⅔ cup Mt. Olive Mild Banana Pepper Rings, coarsely chopped
1 (16-ounce) container sour cream
4 tablespoons southwest seasoning
1 (14.5-ounce) can diced tomatoes with onion, drained
1 cup shredded Cheddar cheese

Combine all ingredients until well blended. Store in air-tight container and refrigerate until ready to serve. Serve dip with nachos if desired.

Mt. Olive Pickles
N.C. Pickle Festival

N.C. Pickle Festival

Last full weekend in April

Downtown Mount Olive
919-658-3113
www.ncpicklefest.org

The N.C. Pickle Festival celebrates the town's best known product—Mt. Olive Pickles. The pickle company serves free pickles all day. Throughout the festival main day on Saturday, pickle-themed events abound. The Pickle Packing Production Challenge gives folks a chance to try their hand at packing pickles and to see how fast they can be, using a real stainless packing table from the pickle company. Not to be missed is the pickle derby, where kids choose a cucumber, rubber band it to a small car or skateboard, and race it down a brightly colored track. The festival also features a one-ring circus, a professional eating competition, and a naturalization ceremony for new citizens from throughout Eastern North Carolina. Enjoy three stages of live entertainment all day, plus the usual assortment of food and crafts vendors, and one of the largest car shows in Eastern North Carolina.

Sharon's Collard Dip

12 ounces cooked, chopped collards
2 (8-ounce) cartons sour cream
2 (4-ounce) cans water chestnuts, chopped
5 ounces shredded cheese, sharp or mild
1 packet Lipton vegetable soup mix

Mix ingredients together in a loaf baking dish. Bake at 350°
for 30 minutes. Serve with crackers or chips of your choice.

North Carolina Cotton Festival

Columbus County Farmers Market

RiverLink's Smoked Trout Dip

1 boneless smoked trout, about 8
   ounces
½ cup cream cheese, softened
½ cup sour cream
1 tablespoon prepared horseradish

1 tablespoon minced red onion
1 tablespoon minced flat-leaf parsley
½ lemon, juiced
4 ribs celery, cut into sticks
1 endive, separated into leaves

Discard fish head and skin; flake the fillets. Purée cream cheese, sour cream, and horseradish in a mini food processor. Add fish and pulse to make a smooth dip. Transfer to a bowl and stir in onion and parsley. Add lemon juice to taste. Refrigerate until firm, about 1 hour. Serve with celery or endive leaves.

RiverLink's RiverFest

Mom's Famous Clam Dip

1 large garlic clove, peeled and split
2 (8-ounce) packages cream cheese, softened
1 tablespoon Worcestershire sauce
1 tablespoon lemon juice
Pinch salt and pepper
2 (6.5-ounce) chopped or minced clams, drained with broth reserved

Rub mixing bowl with garlic; discard garlic. Add to bowl cream cheese, Worcestershire sauce, lemon juice and salt and pepper. Mix until well combined. Add clams and mix until just combined. Add 1 to 2 tablespoons clam broth as needed to achieve desired consistency. Serve with your favorite chips or crackers.

Ann Bokelman, Old Bridge Cookbook
Old Bridge Preservation Society

RiverLink's RiverMusic

May – September

**River Arts District
Asheville**

Each year RiverLink offers 5 Friday night free live music concerts along the French Broad River called RiverMusic. National and local acts perform at the RiverLink Sculpture and Performance Plaza. Check out their website for specific dates.

RiverFest and
Anything That Floats Boat Parade

August

RiverLink also is the proud sponsor of the annual RiverFest and Anything That Floats Boat Parade. This family-friendly event offers lots of fun for the kids, complete with craft booths, hula-hooping, puppies and a Kid's Parade.

It wouldn't be summer without the Anything that Floats Parade. Participants construct vessels out of anything that floats and parade them by the festival grounds. The only rules are they must float and must be powered by wind, solar or herculean human strength—no motors allowed!

Visit www.riverlink.org for specific dates and detailed information on these fun events.

Patty's Crab Dip

1 cup mayonnaise
1 tablespoon Dijon mustard
1 teaspoon lemon juice
½ teaspoon pepper sauce
¼ teaspoon salt
¼ teaspoon cayenne pepper
¼ cup diced bell pepper

¼ cup diced celery
¼ cup diced onion
1 teaspoon garlic powder
1 tablespoon minced, fresh parsley
½ cup grated Parmesan cheese
1 pound jumbo lump crabmeat

Mix all ingredients except crab. Gently fold in crab. Bake at 350° for 40 minutes. Serve with toasted baguette slices.

Recipe courtesy of The Ashford Inn
910-596-0961 • www.ashford-inn.com
Christmas in the City

Christmas in the City

Clinton
910-299-4904
www.downtownclinton.com

Come to downtown Clinton each year for Christmas in the City! There is an old-fashioned community Christmas tree lighting, a gingerbread decorating activity for children, carriage and hay rides around historic downtown Clinton, choirs singing on the Courthouse Square, and a fundraising reception at the Sampson County History Museum. The Sampson County History Museum travels back in time with an onsite old country store, agriculture, civil war, law enforcement, military, and medical exhibits. The Bunting log cabin and Holmes House take you back to a time when Christmas was simple and heartwarming. The Clinton Main Street Program brings this event to downtown each year in partnership with the Sampson County Arts Council, the Sampson County History Museum, the Clinton-Sampson Chamber of Commerce, and the Sampson County Convention and Visitors Bureau.

Chafing Dish Crab

8 ounces crabmeat
2 tablespoons fresh lemon juice
1 teaspoon minced onion
¼ cup half-and-half
Hot sauce to taste

¼ teaspoon Worcestershire sauce
6 ounces cream cheese
¼ cup mayonnaise
¼ cup grated Parmesan cheese

Place crabmeat in top of double boiler. Pour lemon juice over crab. Add remaining ingredients. Heat over boiling water, stirring until mixture is blended. Serve in chafing dish with crackers or toasted bread points.

Graveyard of the Atlantic Museum

Authentic Armenian Eggplant Dip
(Babaghanoush)

2 eggplants, 1½ to 2 pounds each
1 cup tahini
1 cup lemon juice or more to taste
Salt

2 or 3 minced cloves garlic or more to taste
Pita bread

Wash and prick eggplants with fork. Bake in 350°oven until soft, turning periodically. Cool eggplant; remove skin and most of the seeds. Drain eggplant in colander 30 minutes. Cut into chunks and process in food processor until fine.

Add tahini, lemon juice (at least 1 cup), salt and garlic to taste. Best if made a day ahead. Before serving, adjust seasoning with more lemon juice and/or salt and/or garlic to taste. Serve with pita bread triangles.

Karen Joseph, Old Bridge Cookbook
Old Bridge Preservation Society

Out-On-A-Limb Red Apple Salsa

3 cups chopped apples
1 cup of diced tomatoes
1 cup brown sugar
¼ cup of white vinegar
½ cup of chopped green peppers

½ cup of chopped red peppers
½ cup of chopped onions
½ tablespoon of seeded, chopped
   jalapeno peppers (optional)

Combine all ingredients in food processor and process until well blended. Chill, serve with tortilla chips or use to glaze chicken or pork.

John and Joann D'Ambra
Old Cider Mill

Dining Room at Starlight Cafe

Garden Salsa

2 cups chopped tomatoes
⅓ cup chopped yellow onion
2 tablespoons chopped cilantro
2 tablespoons lime juice
1 jalapeño peppers, stemmed, seeded and finely chopped
¼ teaspoon salt

Combine all ingredients in large bowl, toss well. Refrigerate at least 1 hour before serving. Serve with favorite tortilla chips.

Arts Council of Wayne County

102 North John Street • Goldsboro
919-736-3300
www.ArtsInWayne.org
Facebook: artscouncilofwaynecounty

Hours:
Monday through Wednesday 9am to 5pm
Thursday and Friday 9am to 7pm
Saturday 4pm to 7pm

The Arts Council of Wayne County has been providing great arts programming since 1963. Located in historic downtown Goldsboro, the ACWC boasts a very hip facility that houses, galleries, the Art Market, performance space, music and visual arts classrooms, and 8 artist studios. Stop in and see an exhibit, browse the Art Market, take part in Open Mic Night, or enjoy a First Friday celebration. There is always something going on at the Arts Council of Wayne County.

BBQ Jalapeño Poppers

18 fresh jalapeños
1 (8-ounce) package cream cheese, softened
½ cup grated Cheddar cheese
1 green onion, sliced
18 slices thin bacon, cut in half
Barbecue sauce
Toothpicks

Wearing rubber gloves, cut peppers in half lengthwise. Try to keep the stems intact; they look prettier that way. With a spoon, scrape out seeds and light-colored membranes. The heat comes from the seeds and membranes, so if you can handle the heat leave some of them intact.

In a bowl combine cream cheese, Cheddar cheese and green onion. Mix together gently. Stuff pepper halves with cream cheese mixture. Wrap bacon slices around each half, covering as much of the surface as you can. Be careful not to stretch bacon too tightly around peppers as the bacon will contract as it cooks. Brush surface of bacon with your favorite barbecue sauce.

Secure jalapeños with toothpicks, place on baking sheet and pop them into 350° oven for 1 hour or until bacon is cooked and sizzling. Serve hot or at room temperature.

Sonya Snyder, Town of Cary Parks,
Recreation and Cultural Resource Department
Cary Kite Festival

Deliciously Stuffed Sweet Mini-Peppers

1 (8-ounce) package cream cheese,
  softened
½ cup (4-ounces) shredded sharp
  Cheddar cheese
½ cup (4-ounces) shredded Monterey
  Jack cheese
6 ounces hot pork sausage, browned
  and crumbled

¼ teaspoon salt
¼ teaspoon chili powder
¼ teaspoon garlic powder
14 to 16 Bailey's sweet mini-peppers,
  halved
½ cup dry breadcrumbs

In mixing bowl, combine cheeses, sausage and seasonings. Mix well. With spoon, fill each pepper half. Roll in breadcrumbs. Place in greased 15x10x1-inch pan. Bake uncovered at 350° for 20 minutes.

Variation: For a lower calorie version, use low fat cheese and sausage. For a spicy stuffing, add 1 minced jalapeño or habanero pepper to mix.

Courtesy of Bailey's Farms, Oxford
Granville Tourism Development Authority

Granville Tourism Development Authority

124 Hillsboro Street
Oxford
919-693-6125
www.visitgranvillenc.com

Located in the north eastern part of the triangle lies historic Granville County. Known for its hospitality, culture and endless recreational opportunities, Granville County is the place to be. Spend the day on one of five lakes fishing, visit the celebrated Granville County Museum for a look into the county's rich past or simply enjoy a meal on the front porch at Harvest, an esteemed farm to table restaurant.

Granville County plays host to three large events each year. The second Saturday in September the North Carolina Hot Sauce Contest has people flooding the streets of Downtown Oxford for a taste of North Carolina's most popular fiery foods and sauces. The Annual Butner Chicken Pickin' features an abundance of the area's best BBQ Chicken pit masters to see who can take home the grand prize and the Creedmoor Music Festival boasts some of the best artists for an all-day event.

Blueberry Cheese Balls

1½ cups fresh North Carolina
   blueberries
1 cup crushed pineapple, drained
1 red bell pepper, chopped fine
1 tablespoon Lawry's seasoned salt

2 (8-ounce) packages cream cheese,
   softened
2 cups grated smoked Gouda
   cheese
Paprika for dusting

Combine all ingredients except paprika and roll into balls. Roll in paprika. Chill at least 4 hours before serving.

Cindy Carter
North Carolina Blueberry Festival

North Carolina Blueberry Festival

3rd Saturday in June

Burgaw
910-259-2007
www.ncblueberryfestival.com

The North Carolina Blueberry Festival is Burgaw's annual community celebration. Founded in 2004, the Blueberry Festival has become Burgaw's premier event. Held on the third Saturday in June, the Blueberry Festival provides an opportunity for people to enjoy a full day of family entertainment while experiencing the southern hospitality of a small town. More than 30,000 people are estimated to attend the annual one day event. The Festival is a great source of local pride, with the entire community involved in promoting Burgaw to the world in its finest shade of blue. More than 100 volunteers are required to stage over 20 events ranging from entertainment to car show, a street fair, recipe contest, barbeque cook-off, a 5K run, special exhibits, and a variety of other events. There is something for everyone, come join the fun at the North Carolina Blueberry Festival!

Orange and Cranberry Cheese Ball

2 (8-ounce) packages cream cheese, softened
1 cup finely chopped, dried cranberries
1 (11-ounce) can mandarin oranges, drained
1 teaspoon grated orange peel
1 teaspoon vanilla
2 cups chopped pecans, divided

Combine cream cheese, cranberries, mandarin oranges, orange peel, vanilla and 1 cup pecans. Shape into a ball and roll in remaining pecans. Wrap and refrigerate overnight. Serve with butter or vanilla cookies. Wonderful paired with a glass of Laurel Gray Vineyards Pinot Gris or Viognier.

Laurel Gray Vineyards

Cream Cheese Chicken Ball

2 (8-ounce) packages cream cheese, softened
1 package dry ranch dressing mix
1 cup finely chopped chicken meat
1 cup shredded Cheddar cheese

Combine cream cheese and ranch dressing. Add chicken and cheddar cheese. Mix well. Shape into a ball or serve as a spread. Can be served immediately or refrigerated until ready to serve.

Susan Matthews Brown
North Carolina Poultry Jubilee

Cheese Ball

2 (8-ounce) packages cream cheese, softened
2 cups shredded Cheddar cheese
1 tablespoon chopped pimento
1 tablespoon chopped green bell pepper
1 tablespoon chopped onion
1 tablespoon Worcestershire sauce
1 teaspoon lemon juice
¼ teaspoon garlic powder
Dash salt

Mix all ingredients together. Form into ball and chill until ready to serve.

Neuse River Music Fest

Beer Cheese

1 package original Hidden Valley Ranch Dip mix
2 cups shredded Cheddar cheese
2 (8-ounce) packages cream cheese, softened
½ to ¾ cup beer

Mix dip mix with cheeses and slowly add beer until creamy. Chill and serve with pretzels.

Sonya Snyder, Town of Cary Parks,
Recreation and Cultural Resource Department
Cary Kite Festival

Easy Cheese Ball

2 (8-ounce) packages cream cheese, softened
1 large spoonful sour cream
1 (15-ounce) package smoked beef, chopped fine
4 green onion tops, chopped fine
1 (6-ounce) bag finely chopped pecans

Mix together cream cheese, sour cream, smoked beef and onion tops. Roll into a ball and roll in pecans. Refrigerate until ready to serve

Anne Stone
Touch of Heaven Alpacas

The "Rhett" Pimiento Cheese Sandwich

This big, filling sandwich is a customer favorite! Our homemade Pimiento Cheese is the star of this delicious sandwich, perfectly complemented with fresh sprouts, spinach, cucumbers, and crispy bacon. For a vegetarian version, just leave out the bacon.

Pimiento Cheese:

Makes 1½ pounds of delicious Pimiento Cheese. Use on sandwiches or toasted crisps as an appetizer.

¼ pound pepper jack cheese
¼ pound Havarti cheese
½ pound Cheddar cheese
½ pound cream cheese, softened

1 jar pimientos
2 tablespoons jalapeño juice
2 slices jalapeños, finely chopped
1 tablespoon mayonnaise

Combine cheeses in food processor. Transfer to a large bowl, add remaining ingredients and mix well.

Sandwich:

2 slices sun-dried tomato bread
Fresh spinach
Sprouts

5 slices crisp cucumber
2 slices crispy bacon
Red onion slice, optional

To assemble sandwich, spread a thick layer of Pimiento Cheese on 1 slice of bread. Top with spinach, sprouts, cucumber, bacon, onion and remaining slice of bread. Enjoy!

1861 Farmhouse Market

Helpful Hints and Uses of Cheese

- Farmstead and artisan cheeses may be substituted in recipes calling for cheese, lending flavor and sophistication to any meal.

- Fresh goat cheese (Chevre) or fresh cow cheese (fromage blanc) from your local WNC cheesemaker can take the place of cream cheese and/or sour cream in any recipe.

- Use soft goat cheese or herbed goat cheeses in lasagna and other pasta recipes. The soft cheese will melt and combine with the ingredients into a wonderful creamy sauce when you add hot, drained pasta to the bowl.

Aged and fresh goat and cow cheeses are available from WNC Cheese Trail producers, including many cheeses unique to this region of the country.

WNC Cheese Trail

828-458-0088
www.wnccheesetrail.org

The cheesemaking community in WNC is vibrant and growing! Guests can spend an afternoon or a weekend exploring the beautiful mountains of Western North Carolina and sampling some of the best handmade cheese being made in the South today. The trail allows guests to connect directly with cheesemakers to see where their favorite cheeses are crafted and buy straight from the producers. Each producer has a very different story and approach to their craft. The award winning cheesemakers run new operations and are pioneers in the artisan cheese. A current map with new members and new stops on the trail is always available on the website.

Fried Green Tomatoes and Spicy Pimento Cheese

3 medium green tomatoes
1 cup flour, seasoned with garlic powder, onion powder, salt and pepper
2 cups buttermilk
2 cups panko breadcrumbs

Slice tomatoes about ¼ inch thick. Dredge in seasoned flour, shake off excess. Dip in buttermilk. If buttermilk gets too thick from flour add a little water. Gently press in breadcrumbs to ensure even coverage. Pan-fry or deep-fry tomatoes in oil heated to 350°. Drain on paper towels and season with a little salt. Serve with Pimento Cheese. Makes 4 servings.

Pimento Cheese:

1 cup mayonnaise
1 tablespoon Tabasco
1 teaspoon garlic powder
1 teaspoon onion powder

¼ cup Creole mustard
¼ cup diced pimentos
3 cup shredded mild Cheddar cheese

Mix all ingredients except cheese together in mixing bowl. Stir in cheese. Depending on your preference for a creamy or chunky spread, add more cheese if desired. Best if made in advance of use. Makes 4 cups.

Josh's On Union Square • 828-324-5674
Shuck & Peel Party

Fresh Basil, Parmesan and Parma Ham Pinwheels

Serves 12 to 18 for a party or reception at Camp David

1 (8-ounce) package cream cheese, softened
1 ounce fresh oregano
1 cup fresh grated Pecorino Parmigiana cheese or grated, shaker cheese from
    Kraft (small grind, not strings)
6 (10-inch) flour tortilla wraps
12 slices Parma ham, Italian ham or other tasty ham
6 ounces fresh basil or more for basil lovers

Mix cream cheese, oregano and cheese in bowl. Spread each tortilla wrap lightly with cream cheese mixture. Arrange 2 ham slices across the middle of each tortilla. Add a layer of fresh basil leaves.

Starting at one end, tightly roll up each tortilla wrap. Place tortilla rolls in a dish, cover and refrigerate for 2 hours to chill.

Slice each roll creating pinwheels, and serve as soon as possible. The slices on the end are not the best looking (those are snacks for hungry spouses watching you make these). The slices from the middle will be perfect and look great. Make sure your knife is thin and long and razor sharp, otherwise it will crush and ruin the wrap while cutting. You may need to clean the knife occasionally to ensure you are not smearing while cutting the rest of the wraps.

Chef Marti Mongiello of the Inside the Presidents' Cabinet Show,
www.insidethepresidentscabinet.com
Inn of the Patriots

Flat Bread with Caramelized Onion, Blue Cheese and Walnuts

Delicious with a glass of Laurel Gray Cabernet Sauvignon and a couple of good friends.

2 large onions, sliced into thin strips
2 tablespoons extra-virgin olive oil, divided
Salt and pepper to taste
2 tablespoons honey, divided
1 store-bought rolled thin pizza dough
1 (3-ounce) package cream cheese, softened
⅔ cup crumbled blue cheese
1 cup chopped, lightly toasted walnuts

Preheat oven to 450°. In large sauté pan cook onions in 1 tablespoon olive oil until creamy and lightly browned, adding salt and pepper to taste. When cooked, stir in 1 tablespoon honey.

Unroll pizza dough and press out to ½-inch thickness. Brush each side with ½ tablespoon olive oil. Brown each side on a preheated grill pan or griddle. Transfer to a baking sheet. Spread cream cheese over pizza dough and then add blue cheese. Put in hot oven for a couple of minutes until cheeses melt. Top with caramelized onions and walnuts. Drizzle remaining honey over the top. Cut into individual portions and serve warm.

Laurel Gray Vineyards

Veggie Pizza

2 tubes refrigerator crescent rolls
2 (8-ounce) packages cream cheese
1 packet powdered buttermilk ranch dressing
½ cup milk
Vegetables of choice (carrots, broccoli, peppers, tomatoes)

Unroll crescent rolls and place on baking sheet, pressing creases together. Bake at 350° for 10 to 12 minutes until golden brown. Mix together cream cheese, powdered dressing and milk. Spread on the cooled dough. Top with sliced vegetables and refrigerate.

Dr. Mary J. Valenta
Catawba Science Center

Chickpeas with Chouriço Tapas

1 ounce raisins
1 pound Portuguese chouriço
4 tablespoons olive oil
1 large onion, sliced
2 tablespoons parsley

1 clove garlic
2 (14-ounce) cans chickpeas,
   drained
2 tablespoons estate olive oil
¼ pound prosciutto

Hydrate raisins in warm water 10 minutes. Cut sausage into ¼- to ½-inch-thick slices. Heat 4 tablespoons olive oil in saucepan and sauté sausage 5 minutes. Add onion and sauté until clear and tender. Add parsley, drained raisins and garlic. Add chickpeas and stir until warm. Arrange on plate and drizzle estate olive oil over top. Roll up prosciutto and use as garnish around edge of plate. Serve with Silver Coast Winery Touriga and crusty bread. Makes 8 appetizer servings.

Al Gomes
Silver Coast Winery

Watermelon Day at the Greensboro Science Center

Ginger-Glazed Bison Meatballs

Ginger Glaze:

¼ cup cornstarch

½ cup water

1 cup bison broth (Boil bison soup bones in water and use for broth, or
  substitute regular strength beef broth.)

½ cup apple cider vinegar

⅓ cup sugar

1 cup unsweetened pineapple juice

1 tablespoon soy sauce

2 tablespoon grated fresh ginger

Blend glaze ingredients together in a bowl and set aside.

Buffalo Creek Farm and Creamery

Bison Meatballs:

1 (8-ounce) can water chestnuts, drained and chopped

2 eggs, beaten

2 tablespoons soy sauce

2 pounds lean ground bison

¾ cup fine dry breadcrumbs

Olive or cooking oil

In a mixing bowl, blend meatball ingredients together except oil. Mix
thoroughly with fork or your hands. Shape into ¾-inch balls. Place wok
over medium-high heat. When hot, add 1 tablespoon oil. When oil is hot,
add about one third of the meatballs. Stir-fry until well browned, about 8 to
10 minutes. Remove from wok, set aside to drain and brown another batch.
Add more oil as needed and continue until all meatballs are browned. Clean
wok and place over high heat. When wok is hot, pour in Ginger Glaze and
stir until glaze boils vigorously. Add bison balls and simmer 10 minutes.
Serve in electric wok or chafing dish. Makes about 72 cocktail meatballs.

Carolina Bison Farm

Reuben Dip

½ cup mayonnaise
½ cup Thousand Island dressing
16 ounces sauerkraut, rinsed and squeezed dry
8 ounces shredded corned beef
2 cups shredded Swiss cheese

Preheat oven to 350°. In a small bowl, combine mayonnaise and dressing. Spread sauerkraut into a 9x13-inch baking dish. Layer corned beef, Swiss cheese, and the mayonnaise-dressing mixture on top of the sauerkraut. Bake for 20 to 25 minutes.

TheatreNOW

Fried Green Olives

These are so delicious served with a glass of Laurel Gray Cabernet Franc. I like to surprise guests with Fried Green Olives as appetizers with some nice focaccia bread and smoked almonds.

24 pitted green olives	**1 large egg, lightly beaten**
2 ounces blue cheese	**½ cup plain, dried breadcrumbs**
3 tablespoons all-purpose flour	**2 cups vegetable oil**

Soak olives in cold water 15 minutes to reduce brininess. Drain and pat dry. Stuff each with blue cheese. Put flour, egg and breadcrumbs in separate bowls. Dredge olives in flour, dip in egg, and dredge in breadcrumbs. Refrigerate until ready to fry. Heat vegetable oil in saucepan over medium heat until hot but not smoking. Working in batches, fry olives until golden, about 1½ minutes. Transfer to a paper-towel-lined plate using a slotted spoon. Serve warm.

Laurel Gray Vineyards

Laurel Gray Vineyards

5726 Old US Hwy 421
Hamptonville
336-468-9463 (Got Wine)
www.laurelgray.com
www.laurelgraysauces.com

Wednesday through Sunday during February through December

Open Saturdays only in January

Laurel Gray Vineyards is a family farm, owned and operated by Benny and Kim Myers. Their ancestor, Joseph Myers, was the master gardener for England's Queen Charlotte. In 1773, Joseph was given a 400-acre land grant in the current Swan Creek AVA of North Carolina's beautiful foothills. His assignment was to nurture the land and make it productive, a tradition continues today with the family's commitment to excellence at Laurel Gray Vineyards. Winner of many international, regional and local awards, Laurel Gray produces estate grown French wines along with exclusive sauces. Pristine vineyards, a farm pond, and serene porches along with a 1930 renovated milking parlor (tasting room) await for guests arrival. Varieties include Chardonnay, Pinot Gris, Viognier, Merlot, Cabernet Franc, Cabernet Sauvignon, and Petit Verdot.

Summer Cucumber Delights

1 large cucumber, washed
1 (3-ounce) package cream cheese, softened
¼ cup blue cheese salad dressing
1 loaf cocktail rye bread
15 pimento-stuffed green olives, sliced

Slice cucumber into ¼-inch rounds (may be peeled or unpeeled to preference). Set aside. In a small bowl, combine cream cheese and blue cheese dressing; mix well. Spread cheese mixture on rye bread slices. Top with a slice of cucumber and a slice of olive.

Classic Deviled Eggs

6 eggs
¼ cup mayonnaise
1 teaspoon white vinegar
1 teaspoon yellow mustard
⅛ teaspoon salt
Freshly ground black pepper
Paprika, for garnish

Place eggs in single layer in saucepan and add water to cover by 1½ inches. Heat on high until water begins to boil. Cover, turn heat to low and cook 1 minute. Remove from heat and leave covered for 14 minutes. Rinse under cold running water 1 minute. Crack shells and carefully peel under cool running water. Gently dry with paper towel. Slice eggs in half lengthwise, removing yolks to a medium bowl and whites to a serving platter. Mash yolks into a fine crumble with a fork. Add mayonnaise, vinegar, mustard, salt and pepper. Mix well. Evenly disperse heaping teaspoons of yolk mixture into egg whites. Sprinkle with paprika and serve.

North Carolina Poultry Jubilee

Patty's Pretzels

1 heaping tablespoon dill weed
1 heaping tablespoon lemon pepper
1 heaping tablespoon garlic powder
1 package Hidden Valley Ranch dip mix
¾ cup canola oil
1 (16-ounce) bag sourdough pretzels

Combine dry ingredients with oil in measuring cup. Mix well with a spoon. Pour pretzels into large zip-close bag. Add liquid to pretzels and close tight. Marinate for 1 hour, turning occasionally.

Pour pretzel mixture into roasting pan. Bake at 325° for 10 minutes. Cool in pan before serving. I pour them onto a paper towel to drain excess oil before storing in airtight container.

Recipe courtesy of The Ashford Inn
910-596-0961 • www.ashford-inn.com
Christmas in the City

Sangria

1 (12-ounce) can frozen lemonade, thawed
1 (12-ounce) can frozen limeade, thawed
2 (12-ounce) cans frozen white grape/raspberry concentrate, thawed
1 jar cherries with juice
1 cup Sprite
2 cups water
1 bottle Autumn Creek Vineyards Bella Star wine
1 bottle Autumn Creek Vineyards Merlot wine

Mix together and garnish with orange, lemon and lime slices.

Autumn Creek Vineyards

Autumn Creek Vineyards

364 Means Creek Road
Mayodan
336-548-WINE (9463)
www.autumncreekvineyards.com

Autumn Creek Vineyards is nestled in the beautiful rolling countryside of northwestern Rockingham County. With over 100 acres of farmland, 18 acres of grape vines, and picturesque views of the vineyard, Autumn Creek Vineyards is the perfect setting for wine tastings, overnight stays in the cabins, weddings, and all special events. Guests can taste all 12 wines in the 2,000 square-foot Tasting Room and listen to the "Music in the Vines" concert series featuring local artists. There are two incredible log cabins on the edge of the grapevines that are within walking distance of the Tasting Room.

Come experience North Carolina's Wine Country at its best at Autumn Creek Vineyards!

Bat Bite Cocktail

6 ounces warmed apple cider
1½ ounces spiced rum
Splash of cranberry juice
1 cinnamon stick to garnish

Combine all ingredients, mixing well to stir-up your night.
Fireplace optional. Liven up your nocturnal instincts.

John and Joann D'Ambra
Old Cider Mill

Bread & Breakfast

Jalapeño Spoon Cornbread

1 (15.5-ounce) can cream-style corn
1 cup chopped or minced jalapeño
   peppers
⅓ cup oil or melted butter
½ teaspoon baking soda
1 teaspoon salt, optional

¾ cup milk
1 cup cornmeal
2 eggs, lightly beaten
Loads of mozzarella or Cheddar
   cheese, shredded
Paprika, optional

Mix all ingredients except cheese and pour half in a 9x13-inch baking dish. Add a layer of cheese, then remaining batter. Layer top with more cheese and sprinkle with paprika. Bake at 400° for 40 minutes or until done. Check center for doneness; it might be a little soupy because of all the cheese. When done, it will be slightly brown around the edges and on top. Do not overcook.

Doris Thompson
Historic Yates Mill

Honey Corn Puffs

2 cups cornmeal
1 cup flour
1½ teaspoons baking powder
1 teaspoon baking soda
½ teaspoon salt

2½ cups buttermilk or more as needed
2 eggs
¼ cup butter, melted
Honey

Preheat oven to 425° and place baking cups in or grease 12 muffin cups. Mix all dry ingredients together in a large bowl. Add wet ingredients and stir slightly. Allow batter to sit at least 10 minutes. Fill the muffin cups three-quarters full and bake 25 to 30 minutes or until golden brown. Cut a small core from the center of each muffin, cutting about half way down. Add a dollop of honey in the hole and replace core into top of muffins

John Vandenbergh
Historic Yates Mill

Long and Lean Hushpuppies

3½ cups water
2 cups cornmeal
1 teaspoon baking powder
1 tablespoon sugar

1 teaspoon salt
1 medium onion, finely chopped
¼ cup butter or lard, softened

Bring water to a boil. Combine cornmeal, baking powder, sugar, salt and onion; slowly add to boiling water, stirring constantly until mixture is smooth. Remove from heat; add butter, stirring until melted. Cool mixture 10 minutes. Shape batter into 2x1-inch oblong rolls. Deep-fry in hot (375°) oil cooking only a few at a time. Fry until hushpuppies are golden brown. Drain well on paper towels. Serve hot. Makes about 40.

Newport Pig Cooking Contest

Newport Pig Cooking Contest
April

www.newportpigcooking.com

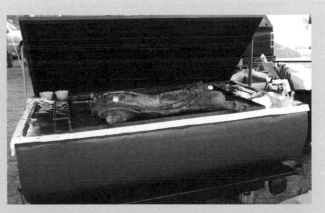

The Pig Cookin' in Newport is a competition of more than 80 cooks all trying to cook a perfect pig and use their secret sauce hoping to be judged #1. There is food, free entertainment, crafts, rides and fun for the whole family. A whole hog is cooked on a large grill, giving Newport the distinction of the largest "Whole Hog Cooking Contest in the USA". There are 10 prizes given to the top chefs. It is a flavor-filled day, but the primary focus is the money raised for the various non-profit charities supported by the Contest. Over $800,000 has been given to these charities, and the number grows every year. To participate in the contest, visit their website for complete information.

Buttermilk Biscuits or Flour Bread

3 cups self-rising flour
¼ cup lard
⅔ cup buttermilk

Buttermilk Biscuits:

Sift flour into bowl in a mound and make a well in the center. Add lard and one third of the buttermilk and mix with hands. Add remaining buttermilk and continue mixing until doughy. Knead dough and cut into round, biscuit-size portions about ½ to 1 inch thick. Bake on ungreased cookie sheet at 425° for 10 to 12 minutes or until brown.

Flour Bread:

Use same process as above but don't cut the dough into biscuit-size portions. Instead, press down enough dough to make a round cake about an inch thick. Put small amount of oil on pan and bake until brown; turn over and brown the other side. Both are good with Grandma's Molasses or chocolate syrup.

Deborah Diane Autry of Autryville
Hollerin' Heritage Festival

Old-Fashioned Biscuits

2 cups self-rising flour
¼ cup cold shortening (may use lard)
1 cup cold buttermilk (may need to adjust amount)
3 tablespoons melted butter

Preheat oven to 450°. Heavily grease a large biscuit pan and set aside. Add flour to large bowl and cut shortening into flour. Add milk and mix with hands, forming light dough. Place dough on floured board and knead just a few times. Flatten to ½-inch thick. Using biscuit cutter, cut dough into biscuits and place in pan. Pour melted butter over each biscuit. Bake 13 to 15 minutes or until golden. Remove from pan and place in covered container; steam 5 minutes. Serve warm.

Ox-Ford Farm

Ox-Ford Farm

75 Ox Creek Road
Weaverville
828-658-2500
www.ox-fordfarm.com

Ox Ford Farm Bed & Breakfast Inn is listed on the National Historic Registry and is part of an authentic working farm located on a slope off the Blue Ridge Parkway near Mount Mitchell. Beef cattle and pedigree sheep are raised on steep mountain pastures with beautiful vistas all around. The history of the farm goes back to 1876, when it was given to a beloved daughter Nancy, who had just married the area's only country doctor. Ox-ford Farm remains today a very special place for the people in the area. The farmhouse is now a bed & breakfast inn, with four full bedrooms and three full baths. Furnishings are beautiful but distinctly comfortable. The atmosphere is very relaxed and homey. Breakfasts are exceptional, made from all naturally grown products including fresh eggs and home-baked bread.

Sweet Potato Biscuits with Johnston County Ham

2 cups Atkinson's Mill Biscuit Mix
¼ teaspoon nutmeg
¼ teaspoon cinnamon
¼ cup cooked and mashed sweet
  potatoes
2 tablespoons brown sugar

5 ounces buttermilk
3 tablespoons melted butter or
  margarine
12 slices Johnston County Cured
  Ham

Preheat oven to 400°. Mix biscuit mix, nutmeg and cinnamon together; set aside. In a separate bowl, mix sweet potatoes, brown sugar, and buttermilk. Stir into dry ingredients to form soft dough. Turn onto lightly floured surface and knead 5 times. Roll to ½-inch thickness; cut with 2-inch biscuit cutter. Bake 12 to 15 minutes or until done. Brush tops of hot biscuits with melted butter or margarine. Pan fry ham slices and fill biscuits. Makes approximately 12 biscuits.

Johnston County Visitors Bureau

Smithfield / Johnston County

Glamour, arts, history, and the great outdoors are all rolled into one in the Smithfield / Johnston County area. The Ava Gardner Museum is home to an incredible collection of photos, costumes, and personal effects of the silver screen legend. The areas calendar of events is filled with local, regional and national acts featured at the Paul A. Johnston Auditorium, Neuse Little Theatre, The Clayton Center or W. J. Barefoot Auditorium. Civil War history in Johnston County is centered on Bentonville Battlefield, the largest battle fought in North Carolina. Also of interest to history buffs are the Johnston County Heritage Center, Benson Museum of Local History and Tobacco Farm Life Museum. Sports and outdoor enthusiasts will find a haven with the six public golf courses, hiking, biking, bird watching, and nature activities at Howell Woods, Clayton River Walk, Buffalo Creek Greenway, and Clemmons State Forest.

Apple Walnut Pull-Apart Bread

2 Granny Smith apples, chopped (peeled or unpeeled)
⅓ cup brown sugar
½ cup walnuts, finely chopped
½ teaspoon cinnamon
12 frozen dinner rolls, thawed
2 tablespoons butter, melted

Preheat oven to 350°. Spray 9x5-inch loaf pan with nonstick cooking spray. Mix together apples, sugar, walnuts and cinnamon until well combined. Using a pair of clean kitchen scissors, cut each roll into thirds. Place 12 roll pieces in bottom of loaf pan. Drizzle about a third of the melted butter on top of roll pieces. Top with a third of the apple mixture. Repeat layers 2 more times, until ingredients are all used up. Let rise about an hour or until rolls have doubled in size. Bake 30 to 35 minutes until tops are golden brown and the middle rolls are done.

Courtesy of the Farmers Market
Historic Morgantown Festival

Graham County Bread

Original recipe from 1865

2 teaspoons baking soda
2 cups buttermilk
3 cups whole wheat flour or 1 cup graham flour and 2 cups whole wheat
1 cup raisins
1 cup brown sugar

Add baking soda to buttermilk and stir until dissolved. Combine flour, raisins and sugar. Add buttermilk and mix until moistened. Place in greased 9-inch round pans or two greased loaf pans and bake at 350° for 35 minutes.

Stecoah Valley Cultural Arts Center

Stecoah Valley Cultural Arts Center

121 Schoolhouse Road
Stecoah (Robbinsville)
828-479-3364
www.stecoahvalleycenter.com

The mission of the Stecoah Valley Cultural Arts Center is to serve the people of Stecoah and Graham County through programs and services that benefit all members of the community, through the preservation and promotion of Southern Appalachian mountain culture and through the restoration of the historic old Stecoah School to its original role as the center of the community. Growing from an abandoned school building just a few short years ago to the vibrant center of the community today, Stecoah Valley Cultural Arts Center now offers over 20 programs to approximately 16,000 people annually. The Center brings music to the mountains through the summer performing arts series An Appalachian Evening, as well as the Annual Harvest Festival and other events. Additionally, the Stecoah Artisans Gallery provides sales promotion and support for local and regional artists. Visit their website for detailed information, the complete calendar of events, and to learn more about the areas rich history.

Ice Cream Bread

1 pint (2 cups) your favorite ice cream, softened
1⅓ cups flour (sifted) added in 3 additions

Stir ice cream and flour together. Pour into greased loaf pan.
Place in cool oven, set to 350° and bake 40 to 45.

Ray Pottery

Ray Pottery

460 Cagle Road
Seagrove
910-428-4292
www.raypottery.com

Ray Pottery is handcrafted in historic
Seagrove where pottery has been
created since the late 1700's. It is
designed to be used in the oven,
microwave, and dishwasher. Each
piece is finished with a beautiful
lead-free glaze. Each design is unique
and one-of-a-kind.

Banana Bread

2½ cups cake flour
1 teaspoon salt
1 tablespoon baking soda

2 cups sugar
1 cup butter, softened 4 eggs
6 ripe bananas

Combine dry ingredients in a bowl. Mix wet ingredients in a separate bowl. Mix dry ingredients into wet. Pour into a loaf pan and bake at 350° for 60 to 70 minutes.

Chef Bill Klein
River House Inn

Peach Bread

4 eggs
1¼ cups oil
2 cups sugar
1 teaspoon vanilla

2 cups self-rising flour
2 teaspoons cinnamon
2 cups sliced peaches

Preheat oven to 350°. In mixing bowl, beat eggs, oil, sugar and vanilla until blended. In another bowl combine flour and cinnamon. Stir mixtures together. Fold in peaches. Bake in large bread pan for 50 minutes or small bread pans for 25 minutes or until a toothpick inserted in center comes out clean.

Shawn Dezern
North Carolina Peach Festival

Sweet Banana Cornmeal Muffins

1½ cups flour
½ cup sugar
½ cup stone ground cornmeal
2 teaspoon baking powder
¼ teaspoon salt
⅔ cup plain yogurt

¼ cup melted butter
3 tablespoons milk
1 large egg
½ teaspoon vanilla extract
1 large banana, peeled and mashed

Combine dry ingredients in a bowl, stirring until well mixed. In a separate bowl, combine yogurt, melted butter, milk, egg, vanilla extract and mashed banana, stirring until well blended. Make a well in dry ingredients and add wet ingredients, stirring just until moist. Using a 12 muffin pan lined with paper or foil cups, divide batter evenly among muffin cups. Bake at 375° for 20 minutes or until a wooden toothpick inserted in the center comes out clean. Cool on a wire rack.

Jeanne Robbins
Yates Mill Associates

Historic Yates Mill

Raleigh
www.yatesmill.org

Yates Mill is a fully restored, circa-1756 gristmill in Raleigh. The mill is listed on the National Register of Historic Places and is the only non-reproduction, operational gristmill of its type in North Carolina and one of just a few in the country. It is the centerpiece of Historic Yates Mill County Park, located a few miles south of downtown Raleigh.

Yates Mill Associates is the guardian of this unique cultural and historic site. YMA was formed in 1989 to restore, preserve and operate the mill, and is solely responsible for funding its upkeep and repair. This all-volunteer, nonprofit organization provides mill tours from March through November, and grinds cornmeal monthly on Yates Mill's antique machinery. The cornmeal is available for sale year-round.

Yates Mill is owned by North Carolina State University, which uses the park as a field research facility. Historic Yates Mill County Park, a 174-acre wildlife preserve, is managed by Wake County Parks, Recreation and Open Space. Park amenities include the A. E. Finley Center for Education and Research, pond boardwalks, overlook docks and hiking trails.

Strawberry Bread

3 cups flour
2 cups sugar
1 teaspoon baking soda
1 teaspoon salt
½ teaspoon cinnamon

4 eggs, beaten
½ cup oil
2½ cups fresh strawberries, chopped
    very fine (or use frozen, sliced
    strawberries)

Combine flour, sugar, baking soda, salt and cinnamon in a large bowl. In a separate bowl, stir together remaining ingredients. Make a well in center of the dry ingredients. Add wet ingredients and stir until smooth. Spoon into 2 greased and floured 9x5x3-inch loaf pans. Bake at 350° for 1 hour.

Ingram's Strawberries
Gross Farms

Gross Farms

1606 Pickett Road
Sanford
www.grossfarms.com
www.facebook.com/pages/Gross-Farms/382601835832
www.twitter.com/GrossFarms

Gross Farms, a North Carolina Century Farm located in Sanford, is an authentic family owned working farm. Over the years the Farm has diversified with the addition of two Agritourism components, the Gross Farms Produce Barn (open late April till the end of July) and Gross Farms Corn Maze and Pumpkin Patch (open late September till the end of October). Currently, Gross Farms actively farms more than 1000 acres. Some of the crops grown include rye, soybeans, milo, corn, wheat, straw, flue-cured tobacco, strawberries, asparagus, sweet corn, peas, produce, and pumpkins.

Cherokee Huckleberry Bread

½ cup butter, melted
1 egg
1 teaspoon vanilla
1 cup sugar
2 cups self-rising flour
1 cup milk
2 cups blueberries or huckleberries

Combine butter, egg, vanilla and sugar. Add flour and milk. Stir in berries. Pour into loaf pan and bake at 350° for 40 minutes.

Qualla Arts and Crafts Mutual

Pumpkin Honey Muffins

1 (15-ounce) can pumpkin purée
1 cup sugar
½ cup honey
2 eggs
2½ cups flour
1 teaspoon baking powder
1 teaspoon cinnamon
1 teaspoon mace
⅓ cup Craisins
⅓ cup chopped pecans

Combine pumpkin, sugar and honey. Add eggs 1 at a time, mixing after each addition until smooth. Sift dry ingredients together; stir into the batter and add remaining ingredients. Pour into greased muffin tins or loaf pan. Bake at 325° for 40 minutes.

Kernersville Honeybee Festival

Blueberry Muffins

2¼ cups all-purpose flour
1½ teaspoons baking powder
½ teaspoon salt
¾ cup sugar
1¼ cups whole milk

1 egg, whisked
⅓ cup oil
1 teaspoon vanilla
1 cup fresh or frozen blueberries

Preheat oven to 350°. Sift flour, baking powder and salt into a mixing bowl. Add sugar and mix well. Whisk wet ingredients in a separate bowl. Gently fold wet into dry. Gently fold in blueberries. Scoop into paper-lined or greased muffin cups. Bake at 350° about 15 minutes or until muffins are firm to the touch. Makes about 12 muffins.

West End Bakery
LEAF Festival

Blueberry Muffins

1 stick butter, softened
1 cup sugar
2 eggs
1 teaspoon vanilla

½ cup milk
2 cups self-rising flour
¼ cup honey, optional
1 cup blueberries, fresh or frozen

Preheat oven to 350°. Line muffin pans with paper liners. Beat together margarine, sugar and eggs until light and fluffy; stir in vanilla, milk and flour. Add honey if using. Fold in blueberries; spoon into paper cups and bake until golden brown, 25 to 30 minutes. The honey gives the muffins a little different taste.

Creedmoor Music Festival

Blueberry French-Toast Muffins

3 eggs
1 cup buttermilk
¼ cup pure maple syrup
1 teaspoon cinnamon
1 (8-ounce) day-old challah bread, cubed
1 box Jiffy blueberry muffin mix
1 cup blueberries
Cinnamon sugar

Mix eggs, buttermilk, maple syrup and cinnamon. Pour over bread. Refrigerate overnight. Preheat oven to 350°. Combine muffin mix with bread mixture and fold in blueberries. Scoop into muffin tins. Top with cinnamon sugar. Bake approximately 40 minutes. Serve warm.

Kourtney McClearn
North Carolina Blueberry Festival

Blueberry-Stuffed French Toast

10 slices white bread, cubed
1 (8-ounce) package cream cheese,
   softened
2 tablespoons honey
¼ cup chopped pecans

1 cup fresh blueberries
8 eggs
1½ cups half-and-half
1 tablespoon cinnamon
½ cup maple syrup

Topping:

Powdered sugar

Maple or syrup of your choice

Spray a 9x13-inch glass pan with nonstick spray. Place half of the cubed bread in bottom. Drop chunks of cream cheese evenly over bread cubes, drizzle with honey and sprinkle with pecans. Put blueberries over this and top with remaining cubed bread. In a large bowl, mix eggs, half-and-half, cinnamon, and maple syrup. Pour over all and let rest 1 hour. Bake in preheated 375° oven 40 to 45 minutes. Just before serving, pour a little more syrup over it and dust with powder sugar.

Courtesy of Oxford Bed and Breakfast at the Olde Parsonage
www.oxfordbedandbreakfastnc.com
Granville Tourism Development Authority

Patty's Texas French Toast

Italian bread or other loaf bread
2 eggs
2 cups heavy cream or half-and-half

2 teaspoons vanilla
Canola oil

Preheat oven to 400°. Slice bread in 1½-inch-thick slices. If loaf is narrow, slice diagonally. Whisk eggs, cream and vanilla. Dip bread slices into egg mixture to coat. Do not soak. Cook in hot canola oil until browned. Drain on paper towels. Place on cookie sheet and bake 6 minutes until puffed. Serve hot with maple syrup.

Recipe courtesy of The Ashford Inn
910-596-0961 • www.ashford-inn.com
Christmas in the City

Caramel-Pecan French Toast

1½ cups firmly packed brown sugar
¾ cup butter
¼ cup plus 2 tablespoons light corn syrup
¾ cup chopped pecans, toasted
10 to 12 (1¾-inch thick) slices French
    bread or baguettes
2½ cups milk or half-and-half

4 eggs, beaten
1 tablespoon vanilla
¼ teaspoon salt
1½ teaspoons cinnamon
3 tablespoons sugar
¼ cup melted butter

Combine first 3 ingredients in medium saucepan. Cook over medium heat, stirring constantly, 5 minutes until bubbly. Pour syrup evenly into lightly greased 9x13-inch pan. Sprinkle with pecans. Arrange bread over pecans. Combine milk, eggs, vanilla and salt. Stir well and pour over bread. Cover and chill at least 8 hours.

Combine cinnamon and sugar and sprinkle over bread. Drizzle with melted butter. Bake uncovered at 350° for 45 to 50 minutes or until golden and bubbly. Serve immediately. Makes 10 servings.

Red Rocker Inn

Peach French Toast

2 tablespoons light corn syrup
½ cup butter
1 cup brown sugar, packed
1½ loaves French bread, thickly sliced on the diagonal
5 eggs
1½ cups milk
1 teaspoon vanilla
¼ teaspoon salt
3 or 4 fresh peaches

In a small saucepan combine syrup, butter and brown sugar. Simmer until syrupy. Pour into a 9x13-inch glass baking pan. Place bread slices on the syrup in the baking pan. You will have 2 even layers.

In a large bowl, beat together eggs, milk, vanilla and salt. Pour evenly over bread. Cover and refrigerate overnight. In the morning, preheat oven to 350°. While oven heats, peel and slice peaches. Lift up top row of bread and insert a layer of peach slices. Bake uncovered 45 minutes until golden on top. Cut bread apart and serve immediately with maple or peach syrup.

Johnson's Peaches

Amy's Hearty Pancakes

1 cup Old Mill of Guilford
    Buttermilk Whole Wheat
    Pancake Mix
3 eggs

1 cup plain yogurt
1 cup cottage cheese
1 cup blueberries (optional)

Mix ingredients together. Pour batter onto hot griddle. Flip when small bubbles appear and cook another minute. Serve warm with butter and maple syrup.

Old Mill of Guilford

Old Mill of Guilford

Working Mill and Country Store

1940 Highway 68N
Oak Ridge
336-643-4783
www.oldmillofguilford.com

Open 7 days a week 9am to 5pm

Established in 1767, The Old Mill of Guilford was founded in North Carolina on Beaver Creek in 1767 to grind grain for the early settlers of what is now Guilford County. Today, the mill continues to produce all-natural, stone-ground, whole grain foods, just as it has for over 240 years. The Mill produces all natural corn meal, grits and flour along with a wide range of mixes including: Gingerbread Mixes, Muffin Mixes, Pancake Mixes, Cookie Mixes, Scone Mixes, Biscuit Mixes and Hushpuppy Mix. The Mill's signature mix is the Sweet Potato Muffin. Visit the Old Mill Store for these products and other fine foods and crafts from North Carolina. The Old Mill of Guilford is a popular, scenic tourist attraction and has long been a favorite subject for artists and photographers. So, please make plans to stop by and visit.

Pancakes

2 cups self-rising flour
2 tablespoons sugar
1 egg

1½ cups milk
⅓ cup oil

Mix all ingredients together and cook on hot griddle, flipping once. Makes 12 small pancakes

Qualla Arts and Crafts Mutual

Apple Pancakes

2¼ cups sifted plain flour
5 teaspoons baking powder
1 teaspoon salt
1 teaspoon cinnamon
½ teaspoon nutmeg
3 tablespoons sugar, honey or maple syrup
1 teaspoon vanilla

2 cups buttermilk
6 tablespoons cooking oil
2 eggs, beaten
2 cups finely chopped or grated unpeeled tart apples
½ cup chopped pecans or walnuts, optional

Sift together dry ingredients including sugar. If using honey or maple syrup, add to eggs along with vanilla, buttermilk and oil, beating until smooth. Mix dry and wet ingredients together. Fold in apples and nuts. Spoon onto moderately hot griddle; flip pancakes over once after browning on first side. Serve with butter and syrup or just sprinkle a little powdered sugar on top.

Ann Jackson Garwood
Brushy Mountain Apple Festival

Homemade Butter

Gather cream from the milk you have gotten from your cow for several days. Put it in your churn and let it set out for several days until it comes together. When you lean the churn, the cream sticks together and is very thick. Put the dasher in the churn and churn with quick up and down strokes until butter is formed. Place in a bowl and press together to remove excess milk. Salt to taste.

Alternate method:

If no cow is available, purchase a carton of heavy whipping cream. Pour into a glass jar. Put lid on tightly and shake until butter forms. It may take up to 10 minutes. It will first be fluffy like whipped cream. Then the butter will come together and separate from the milk. Salt to taste.

Denise Jackson of Spivey's Corner
Hollerin' Heritage Festival

Hollerin' Heritage Festival

2nd Saturday in September

Spivey's Corner
www.nationalhollerincontest.com

Each year the "almost lost" art of Hollerin', which is the first form of long distance, farm to farm communication, is revived in Spivey's Corner. The National Hollerin' Contest began in in 1969 and has received worldwide acclaim. Come

join the fun for a day that will include live music, a BBQ cook-off, great food, antique farm equipment displays and demonstrations, living history exhibits, a classic car show, a kid's entertainment zone, craft vendors, and of course, the National Hollerin' Contest. The proceeds from this event have benefited the Spivey's Corner Volunteer Fire Department since its beginning, and it remains the department's sole fundraiser. Lawn chairs, blankets and "sunbrellas" are welcome; no coolers please.

Allspice Apple Butter

3 pounds apples, peeled, cored and cut into ½-inch chunks
1 (16-ounce) box light brown sugar
2 teaspoons cinnamon
1 teaspoon allspice, preferably freshly ground

Place apples in large, heavy-bottom pot over low heat. Cook, uncovered, 1½ hours, stirring occasionally. Add brown sugar and spices. Continue cooking over low heat, stirring occasionally, until very thick, about 30 minutes. To test for doneness, place a spoonful on a white plate and let sit 20 seconds. If a ring of liquid forms around the apples, there is still too much liquid in the mixture. Continue cooking and testing until no ring forms.

Riverlink's RiverFest

Freezer Strawberry Jam

2 cups washed, crushed strawberries, about 1 quart whole berries
4 cups sugar
¾ cup water
1 (1¾-ounce) box powdered fruit pectin

Place crushed berries into large bowl. Add sugar and mix well. Let stand 10 minutes. Mix water and pectin in small saucepan, bring to a boil and boil for 1 minute stirring constantly. Remove from heat and stir into the fruit. Continue stirring 3 minutes. Ladle quickly into sterilized freezable jars, leaving ½-inch headroom. Seal immediately with sterilized tight-fitting lids. Let jars stand at room temperature until jam is set. Freeze. Makes 5 to 6 (8-ounce) jars.

Gross Farms

Peach Jalapeño Jam

4 cups puréed peaches
2½ cups seeded, puréed
   jalapeños

6 cups sugar
1 cup apple cider vinegar
2 packs liquid pectin

Combine peaches, jalapeños, sugar and vinegar in large saucepan. Bring to boil, reduce heat and simmer 10 minutes. Add pectin; increase heat and bring to a rapid boil. Boil 5 minutes. Ladle into sterilized jelly jars and process in boiling-water bath 10 minutes. Let cool until set.

Lisa Rolan
North Carolina Peach Festival

ISTOCK/HAYATIKAYHAN

North Carolina Peach Festival
3rd Saturday in July

Candor

The North Carolina Peach Festival began in 1997, and it gets bigger and better every year. Beginning at 10am with the opening parade, the event hosts 7000 attendees. There is live entertainment, plenty of local peaches, peach ice cream, and peach desserts. The Peachy 5K race is held the Friday before and is always a fun event for the whole family. So come on to Candor's Fitzgerald Park, put out the chairs and enjoy a beautiful, relaxing day filled with fun, food and family.

Lavender-Thyme Jelly

3½ cups water
½ cup dried lavender
¼ cup lemon juice

1¾ ounces powdered pectin
4 cups sugar
½ teaspoon fresh thyme leaves

Boil water in a medium saucepan. Remove from heat and steep lavender for 20 minutes.

Strain out the lavender and pour liquid back into saucepan. Add lemon juice and pectin, stirring until dissolved. Bring mixture to a boil. Add sugar and stir to combine. Return to a boil and cook 4 to 5 minutes. If the mixture is not thick enough, add a little more pectin. Remove from heat and stir in the fresh thyme leaves. Let cool to room temperature and then refrigerate, uncovered, until completely cool. Cover tightly and keep refrigerated. Spread on any type of bread or pastry. It is especially tasty on a sandwich made with sprouted grain or whole-wheat bread, roasted turkey breast, Havarti or Brie cheese, thinly sliced red onion and lettuce.

Chef Denise Gordon
TheatreNOW

Green Chile & Cheese Breakfast Casserole

15 eggs
3 egg whites
¾ cup flour (for gluten free, use
   Bob's Red Mill gluten-free flour)
1½ teaspoons baking powder
3 (8-ounce) cans diced green chiles
1 quart plus 1 pint cottage cheese

2 (8-ounce) packages cream cheese,
   softened
3 (8-ounce) bags shredded
   Monterey Jack cheese
Salt and pepper to taste
12 sausage patties, crumbled
   (optional)

Beat eggs and egg whites lightly in a large bowl. Stir in remaining ingredients, mixing well. Pour into greased 15x11-inch baking pan. Bake 15 minutes at 400° then turn down to 350° and bake 45 minutes longer or until casserole is set.

For a 9x13-inch pan:

10 eggs
2 egg whites
½ cup flour
1 teaspoon baking powder
2 (8-ounce) cans diced green chiles
1 quart cottage cheese
1 (8-ounce) package cream cheese,
   softened

2 (8-ounce) bags shredded
   Monterey Jack cheese
Salt and pepper to taste
8 sausage patties, crumbled
   (optional)

Mix as above. Bake 10 minutes at 400° and about 40 minutes at 350° until set.

The Sunset Inn

Apple Ham Frittata

4 small new potatoes	1 small red onion, divided
8 eggs	Cooked sliced ham
¼ cup half-and-half	Aged white Cheddar cheese
1 teaspoon salt	1 apple, divided
½ teaspoon freshly ground pepper	1 tablespoon minced parsley
¼ teaspoon nutmeg	Zest and juice of ½ lemon

Preheat oven to 350°. Wash potatoes and remove any large eyes. Place in zip-close bag and seal, leaving a small opening. Microwave potatoes for 5 minutes on high. Being careful of hot steam, finish zipping the bag and let potatoes come to room temperature. They can be refrigerated overnight.

In small bowl, whisk together eggs, half-and-half, salt, pepper and nutmeg. Set aside.

Lightly spray 4 (8-ounce) ceramic tart baking dish with nonstick spray. Thinly slice potatoes and cover bottom of each dish. Thinly slice the onion, reserving a few slices, and layer over potatoes. Cut ham into bite-sized pieces and layer over onion. Finely shred cheese and sprinkle approximately ¼ to ⅓ cup over ham. Peel and core the apple. Finely slice apple, reserving a few slices, and place in a single layer over the cheese. Pour egg mixture over layers. You may have to do this a little at a time and wait a minute for it to settle into the layers as the dish will be full. Bake at 350° for 30 minutes.

While dish is baking, finely chop reserved onion and apple and mix with parsley. Add the lemon zest and juice, and combine to make a fine gremolata, which adds a bright flavor and looks pretty as well. Sprinkle frittatas with gremolata before serving.

Note: All steps of this preparation, up to but not including peeling the apple, can be done the night before. When ready to cook, simply assemble and bake.

Haywood County Apple Harvest Festival

Farmer's Quiche

½ stick butter
3 cups frozen hash browns or peeled and diced fresh potatoes
¾ cup chopped red and/or green pepper
¾ cup chopped scallions
1 cup diced baked ham, browned sausage or cooked and crumbled bacon
1 (4-ounce) can mushroom pieces or ½ cup chopped fresh mushrooms
1 cup shredded cheese
3 eggs
½ cup milk

Melt butter in a 9x13-inch glass baking dish. Add potatoes, peppers and scallions. Bake at 350° until tender. Layer meat, mushrooms and cheese on top. Mix eggs and milk; pour over top. Bake at 350° about 30 minutes or until egg mixture is set.

Lazy O Farm

Lazy O Farm

3583 Packing Plant Road • Smithfield
919-934-1132
www.facebook.com/pages/Lazy-O-Farm/124542400961276

This traditional tobacco farm has been in the Olive family since 1850 with the fifth generation working it and the sixth generation growing up on it now. A small section of the 500-acre farm is dedicated to farm education for all ages. A visit to the farm provides one of the best fun-filled educational adventures found anywhere, offering a look at how farming touches every aspect of our lives. Providing food is the most obvious, but visitors may be surprised at the many other agricultural connections there are.

Lazy O Farm offers seasonal adventures that are stuffed with lots of good old fashioned fun and awesome animals. Browse through the Bone Room, mosey around the maze, walk through the soil tunnel and dig into a bucket of fossils and gemstones. Enjoy a hayride around the farm, egg hunts in the spring and pumpkin patch in the fall. Learn how to make ice cream and butter, how a chick hatches, and what a seed does underground. After all the excitement, settle down for a refreshing picnic under the shelter.

Tennessee Pride Hashbrown Casserole

1 (28-ounce) bags O'Brien hash browns, thawed
12 sausage patties, cooked and crumbled
24 ounces sour cream
16 ounces Dean's or Heluva Good french onion dip
1 (10¾-ounce) can cream of chicken soup
6 eggs, beaten
4 cups shredded cheese

Mix all ingredients together and put in greased 11x15-inch glass baking dish. Bake at 350° for 45 minutes and then cover with foil and bake an additional 45 minutes.

For a 9x13-inch pan:

1 (28-ounce) bag O'Brien hash browns, thawed
8 sausage patties, cooked and crumbled
12 ounces sour cream
12 ounces Dean's or Heluva Good french onion dip
1 (10¾-ounce) can cream of chicken soup
5 eggs, beaten
2 cups shredded cheese

Mix and bake as above, slightly reducing baking times.

The Sunset Inn

Soups & Salads

Drunken Sweet Potato Soup

2 large sweet potatoes
1 cup Starrlight Mead Semi-sweet
    Traditional Mead
2 cups apple cider

2 teaspoons cinnamon
1 teaspoon nutmeg
Pinch saffron, optional

Heat oven to 350°. Wrap sweet potatoes in foil and bake 1½ hours. Unwrap and remove skin. Place sweet potatoes in food processor and pulse until small pieces. Add potatoes to soup pot along with mead and apple cider. Cook over medium heat until heated through. If too thick, stir in a little more apple cider to desired consistency. Add spices and optional saffron. Stir and serve.

Note: Apple juice or Starrlight Mead Spiced Apple Mead may be substituted for apple cider.

Robin Floyd, employee
Starrlight Mead

Brushy Mountain Apple Festival

Butternut Squash and Apple Soup

2 tablespoons butter
1 very large onion, chopped
3 stalks celery, sliced caddy-cornered to make it look interesting
2 heaping tablespoons curry powder
1 heaping tablespoon honey
4 to 5 large apples of your choice, peeled and chopped
8 cups butternut squash, peeled and coarsely chopped
8 cups chicken stock
1 teaspoon salt
1 teaspoon black pepper

Melt butter over medium heat in large soup pot. Add onion, celery, curry powder and honey; sauté for 3 minutes. Stir in apples and squash. Add chicken stock, salt and pepper. Bring to a boil, reduce heat and simmer about 35 minutes or until squash is tender. If you want to make it look really fancy, after you put it in soup bowls, sprinkle a little freshly ground pepper or nutmeg on top.

Ann Jackson Garwood
Brushy Mountain Apple Festival

Gazpacho Sharon

1 avocado
1 (29-ounce) can tomato purée
¼ cup olive oil
1 tablespoon minced garlic
1 cup tomato juice
2 teaspoons balsamic vinegar
1 tablespoon Worcestershire sauce
Juice of 1 lime
2 tablespoons freshly ground black pepper
1 tablespoon salt
1 cucumber, peeled, seeded and cut into small pieces
1 medium onion, diced
2 small peppers (1 yellow and 1 red), diced
1 (14-ounce) can diced tomatoes
¼ cup fresh basil, sliced in thin strips
¼ cup fresh parsley, sliced in thin strips
⅛ cup cilantro, sliced in thin strips
Texas Pete hot sauce to taste

In a blender, purée avocado with tomato purée. Add olive oil, garlic, tomato juice, vinegar, Worcestershire sauce, lime juice and salt and pepper; blend. Pour into a large, non-metallic serving bowl and fold in remaining ingredients. Chill 4 to 6 hours. Serve with Silver Coast Viognier .

Note: To enhance presentation, cut additional avocados in half, peel and remove pit. Fill cavity with spiced medium shrimp and float in gazpacho.

Al Gomes
Silver Coast Winery

Mead and Mushroom Soup

2 cups fresh mixed wild mushrooms (shiitake, portobello, cremini, porcini,
  oyster)
1 tablespoon extra virgin olive oil
¼ pound (1 stick) plus 1 tablespoon unsalted butter, divided
1 cup chopped yellow onion
1 carrot, chopped
1 spring fresh thyme plus 1 teaspoon minced thyme leaves, divided
6 cups water
Kosher salt and fresh cracked black pepper
2 cups chopped leek, white and light green parts only
¼ cup all-purpose flour
1 cup Starrlight Mead Off-dry Traditional Mead
1 cup half-and-half
1 cup heavy cream
½ cup minced fresh flat-leaf parsley

Clean mushrooms. Separate and coarsely chop stems. Slice mushroom caps ¼ inch thick (bite size), and set aside.

To make the stock, heat olive oil and 1 tablespoon butter in large pot. Add chopped mushroom stems, onion, carrot, thyme sprig, 1 teaspoon salt and ½ teaspoon pepper. Cook over medium-low heat 10 to 15 minutes until vegetables are soft. Add water and bring to a boil. Reduce heat and simmer, uncovered, 30 minutes. Strain and reserve liquid. You should have 4½ cups stock. If not, add water to make up the difference. Meanwhile, in another large pot, heat remaining butter and add leeks. Cook over low heat 15 to 20 minutes until leeks begin to caramelize. Add flour and cook 1 minute. Add mead and stir another minute, scraping bottom of pan to release browned bits. Add mushroom stock, minced thyme leaves, 1½ teaspoons salt and 1 teaspoon pepper and bring to a boil. Reduce heat and simmer 15 minutes. Add half-and-half, cream and parsley, and season with salt and pepper to taste. Heat through but do not boil. Serve hot with crusty bread and a crisp salad, and the rest of your bottle of mead.

Jenn Hansen, employee
Starrlight Mead

Billi Bi (Mussel Soup) with Curry

This is one of the most heavenly soups you'll ever taste.

2 pounds mussels
¾ cup white wine
1 leek
1 medium yellow onion
1 teaspoon butter
Salt and white pepper to taste
1 clove garlic, peeled and degermed (remove center of clove)
2 medium Yukon gold potatoes, peeled and diced
1 bouquet of thyme, bay and parsley sprigs
2⅓ cups heavy cream, divided
1 teaspoon curry powder

Clean mussels and steam open in wine. Strain and reserve cooking liquid. Pull mussels from their shells and set aside. Coarsely chop leek and onion and sweat in butter. Add salt and white pepper to taste. Once those have softened, add garlic and allow it to sweat. Add potatoes and the herb bouquet and stir around until well incorporated. Add 1⅔ cups cream and reserved mussel-wine liquid and bring to a boil. Reduce heat and simmer until potatoes are tender. While soup is cooking, whip remaining ⅔ cup cream with curry powder until firm. Refrigerate until ready to serve. When potatoes are tender, remove herb bouquet. Place soup in a blender and blend until smooth. For best texture, press soup through a chinois or fine sieve. To serve, ladle soup into bowls, drop in a few mussels and top with a dollop of curry cream. Makes 4 servings.

Chef Bill Klein
River House Inn

Kickin' Bean & Walnut Soup

3 (15-ounce) cans Great Northern Beans
   (do not drain)
2 (14.5-ounce) cans diced tomatoes
   (do not drain)
½ cup sliced carrots
½ cup chopped onions
½ cup chopped green peppers
1 cup chopped walnuts, divided
1 cup crisp bacon bits, divided
¼ jar chili powder or to taste
3 tablespoons hot sauce or to taste
1 to 2 cups shredded Cheddar cheese

Combine beans, tomatoes, carrots, onions, and green peppers in large pot. Mix well and heat over medium-high heat. Add ½ cup chopped walnuts and ½ cup crisp bacon bits. Stir well and bring to simmering boil. Reduce heat to low simmer. Add chili powder and hot sauce. Stir well. Simmer at least 1 hour. However, the longer it can simmer the more the flavors blend into perfection. Stir every 5 to 10 minutes and be sure that it is not getting too hot or too dry. If it starts to boil, reduce heat. If it gets too dry add a can of tomato sauce. Serve garnished with reserved walnuts and bacon bits and top with Cheddar cheese. Delicious with a crisp salad.

Sheffield Mine

Delicious Taco Soup

1 pound ground beef
1 small onion, chopped
1 (4-ounce) can chopped green
  chilies
1 (15-ounce) can Ranch-style
  beans
1 (15-ounce) can whole kernel
  corn

1 (14.5-ounce) can stewed
  tomatoes
1 (10-ounce) can Rotel tomatoes
1 cup water
1 envelope dry ranch dressing
  mix
1 envelope taco seasoning mix

Brown ground beef with onion and green chilies; drain. In large pot, combine ground beef with remaining ingredients. Simmer 30 minutes. Delicious served alone or on top of tortilla chips and garnished with sour cream and shredded Cheddar cheese.

Denton Farm Park

Denton FarmPark

**1072 Cranford Road
Denton
336-859-2755**

Denton FarmPark encompasses 160-plus acres, complete with a railroad called the "Handy Dandy" that circles the Park on 1½ mile track. There are fifteen restored old buildings on site; a church, a general store, radio museum, grist mill, shoe shop, machine shop, doll museum, and plantation buildings. Nature lovers can enjoy over 500 campsites and with permanent restroom facilities. The Park is also a special event venue for private functions such as company picnics, weddings, and scouting events. The Park is open by appointment only.

Ground Beef Vegetable Soup

1 pound ground beef
1 quart stewed tomatoes with pepper and onions
5 (8-ounce) cans tomato sauce
5 cups water
3 teaspoons sugar
1 (10-ounce) package frozen mixed vegetables
1½ envelope dry onion soup mix

Brown ground beef and drain well. Combine remaining ingredients with beef into large soup pot. Simmer 1 to 2 hours. The flavor enhances the longer it is allowed to simmer. Add an additional 8 ounce can tomato sauce and 1 cup water if simmering for longer than 1½ hour.

Denton Farm Park

Annual Events at Denton FarmPark

Military Vehicle and Collector Show
2nd weekend in April

**The Doyle Lawson and Quicksilver's
Bluegrass Music Festival**
The 3 days before Mother's Day in May

**Antique Motorcycle Club of America's
Southern National**
3rd weekend in May

Southeast Old Threshers' Reunion
5 days including the 4th of July

Dailey Vincent Fest
3rd weekend in September

Country Christmas Train weekends
Beginning the Saturday after Thanksgiving and each
weekend thereafter until Christmas

BLT Soup

¼ cup butter
¼ cup flour
4 cups chicken stock
2 cups half-and-half
8 slices bacon

1 teaspoon ham base*
Dash nutmeg
2 medium tomatoes, peeled and
   diced
1 cup chopped iceberg lettuce

Melt butter in top of double boiler over direct heat. Add flour and stir 1 minute while it bubbles. Add chicken broth and mix well with whisk. Leave over direct heat, stirring frequently until thickened. Add half-and-half. Put water in bottom of double boiler and place top half over bottom half. Reduce heat to low.

Cook bacon, reserve bacon drippings. Add 1 tablespoon bacon drippings to soup and mix well. Add ham base, nutmeg and tomatoes. Taste and add salt if necessary. Cover and simmer gently over, not in, boiling water, for 20 minutes. Just before serving add chopped lettuce and bacon.

*Ham base, or ham flavoring, can usually be found with the soups in a well-stocked grocery store. If you can't find it, use a little extra bacon and substitute some of the bacon grease for butter in the first step.

Fryemont Inn

Carmel's Goat Cheese-Tomato Bisque

2 tablespoons butter
1 medium sweet onion, chopped
½ teaspoon salt
1 (28-ounce) can diced tomatoes
3 tablespoons prepared basil pesto

½ cup crumbled goat cheese
1 tablespoon honey
2 teaspoons balsamic vinegar
Fresh ground black pepper to taste

Melt butter in a 4-quart saucepan over medium heat. Add onion and sauté until translucent and tender. Add salt and tomatoes along with their liquid and bring to a slow simmer. Add pesto, goat cheese, honey and vinegar. Stir until cheese is melted.

Remove from heat and using an immersion blender, purée until smooth. Add pepper to taste. If you prefer a thinner soup add ¼ to ½ cup of hot water and adjust salt and pepper. Garnish with a perfect miniature grilled cheese sandwich and enjoy! Makes approximately 4 cups.

Grove Arcade

Potato Soup

3 cups diced potatoes
½ cup diced celery
½ cup diced onion
1½ cups water
2 chicken bouillon cubes

½ teaspoon salt
2 tablespoons flour
½ cup sour cream
2 cups milk
1 teaspoon chopped chives, optional

Combine potatoes, celery, onion, water, bouillon cubes and salt. Bring to a boil. Reduce heat and simmer until potatoes are tender. Mix flour with sour cream and stir into soup along with milk. Reheat to gentle simmer. Do not boil. Serve garnished with chives.

Qualla Arts and Crafts Mutual

Corn and Potato Chowder

4 medium potatoes
½ teaspoon salt
¼ cup chopped onion
3 cups water
2 (10½-ounce) cans chicken broth
3 cups whole-kernel corn
¾ stick salted butter
1 (12-ounce) can evaporated milk
4 cups whole milk
1 (10-ounce) can Rotel Original Diced Tomato and
    Green Chiles
½ teaspoon black pepper
1 pound Velveeta cheese, cut into 1-inch cubes

Combine potatoes, salt, onion, water and chicken broth in a tall soup pot. Cook at slow boil until potatoes are tender. Add corn and return to slow boil. Cook an additional 10 minutes. Add butter, evaporated milk, whole milk, Rotel tomatoes and black pepper. Simmer on medium-low until heated through. Add cheese and continue to cook on low until all cheese is melted. Yummy with a glass of Laurel Gray Vineyards Chardonnay and a warm piece of homemade cornbread.

Laurel Gray Vineyards

Shrimp and Corn Chowder

2 teaspoons coarse salt, plus more for cooking water
10 ears fresh corn
4 tablespoons unsalted butter
2 large sweet onions, finely chopped
½ cup all-purpose flour
1 teaspoon fresh ground pepper
½ teaspoon turmeric
2½ quarts low-sodium chicken broth
1½ pounds potatoes, unpeeled, cut into ½-inch slices
¼ cup white wine, optional
1 cup fat-free evaporated milk
½ pound white Cheddar cheese, grated
1 pound shrimp, peeled, deveined and cut into 1-inch pieces
Chives, cut into ¼-inch lengths for garnish

Bring a medium pot of salted water to a boil. Add corn and blanch 3 minutes. Drain and set aside.

Melt butter in medium stockpot over medium heat. Add onions and cook, stirring frequently, until translucent, 10 to 15 minutes. Add flour, salt, pepper and turmeric and cook, stirring, about 3 minutes. Add chicken broth and potatoes. Bring to a boil and simmer until potatoes are tender, about 15 minutes. Add optional wine and simmer another 5 minutes.

Remove corn kernels from ears. You should have about 6 cups. Add corn, evaporated milk, cheese and shrimp and cook until shrimp are pink and cooked through, 3 to 4 minutes. Serve hot, garnished with chives.

Mebane Stolfi, Old Bridge Cookbook
Old Bridge Preservation Society

Two Bean Chowder with Pesto

8 ounces dried great Northern beans
8 ounces dried pinto beans
10 cups water, divided
2 cups chopped cauliflower
2 medium carrots, shredded
1 medium parsnip, peeled and diced
1 medium leek, chopped
1 teaspoon salt
1 teaspoon instant vegetable or chicken bouillon granules
1 teaspoon dried oregano, crushed
1/2 teaspoon marjoram, crushed
2 bay leaves
1/4 teaspoon pepper
2 cups milk
6 tablespoons pesto

Rinse dried beans and combine in a Dutch oven with 6 cups water. Bring to a boil, reduce heat and simmer 2 minutes. Remove from heat. Cover and let stand 1 hour. Drain and rinse beans.

In Dutch oven combine beans, 4 cups water, cauliflower, carrots, parsnip, leek, salt, bouillon, oregano, marjoram, bay leaves and pepper. Bring to a boil. Reduce heat, cover and simmer 1½ to 2 hours or until beans are tender, stirring occasionally. Discard bay leaves. Mash beans slightly. Stir in milk and heat through. Season to taste with salt and pepper.

Ladle chowder into 6 individual bowls and swirl 1 tablespoon pesto on top of each bowl.

Emily Shea, Old Bridge Cookbook
Old Bridge Preservation Society

Rabbit Stew

1 (3-pound) rabbit, cut up or whole
1 cup chopped celery
1 large onion, chunked
1 bay leaf
4 cups water
4 cups Starrlight Off-dry Blackberry Mead

2 cups carrots, diced
4 medium red potatoes, chunked
4 ounces sliced mushrooms, sautéed
¼ cup all-purpose flour or corn starch
⅓ cup water
Salt and pepper to taste

Add rabbit, celery, onion, bay leaf, water and mead to a crockpot. Cook on low 4 hours. Add carrots, potatoes and mushrooms an hour before serving and cook until vegetables are tender. Remove bay leaf. Combine flour and water; stir until well blended and smooth. Stir flour mixture into broth, stirring until thickened. Salt and pepper to taste. Makes 4 to 6 servings.

Becky Manda, employee
Starrlight Mead

Starrlight Mead

When people think of Mead, or honey wine, the heart of central North Carolina is probably not the first thing that comes to mind. Renaissance Fairs, Vikings or old English castles are probably what the mind conjures. Starrlight Mead hopes to change that. Opened in September 2010 and using local NC honey, Starrlight Mead is crafting award winning meads to surprise and delight both mead drinkers and wine lovers alike. "Most people assume that all mead is sweet, since it is made with honey, but you might be surprised!" says Becky Starr, owner. With over 15 varieties available, several are off-dry, or lightly sweet, and others range from semi-sweet to sweet. Traditional Mead, honey diluted with water and then fermented, derives its flavor from wildflower honey and is available in two sweetness levels. Other varieties, flavored with fruit juice such as Blackberry, Spiced Apple, and Peach, are also available, along with seasonal treats.

Spicy Peanut Stew

2 dry chili peppers
¼ teaspoon dry parsley flakes
½ teaspoon dry onion flakes
½ teaspoon dry garlic flakes
¼ teaspoon dry coriander

1 cup dry vegetable powder
1 teaspoon dry chili powder
¼ teaspoon Hungarian paprika
6 cups water

Mix above soup base ingredients in a large pot and bring to a boil. Cover partially and simmer 25 minutes.

2½ pounds spinach, stemmed
3 tablespoons vegetable oil
½ onion, chopped
1 Scotch Bonnet pepper, seeded and
   minced (careful, this one is hot!)
6 large scallions, coarsely chopped
4 large garlic cloves, minced
2 large sprigs thyme

1 large green bell pepper, diced
1 tablespoon minced fresh ginger
1 teaspoon ground allspice
Salt and freshly ground pepper
½ cup crushed, blister-fried Baker
   Peanuts or ½ cup Cajun-dusted
   crushed peanuts

Heat saucepan. Rinse spinach; add handfuls to saucepan and wilt. Transfer to food processor and coarsely purée.

In the same pot, heat the oil. Add onion, Scotch bonnet, scallions, garlic, thyme, bell pepper, ginger and allspice. Cover and cook until vegetables are softened. Add the above soup base and bring to a boil. Cover partially and simmer 25 minutes. Add spinach purée and simmer 5 minutes. Discard thyme and dried chili peppers. Season with salt and pepper to taste and serve with crushed peanuts

Bakers' Southern Traditions

Foothills Chicken Stew

6 to 7 bone-in chicken breasts
2 tablespoons crushed red pepper
   flakes
1 stick butter

2 cups milk
3 tablespoons cornstarch
1 tablespoon salt
Black pepper to taste

Place chicken and red pepper in Dutch oven. Fill with water to three-quarters full. Cook until chicken falls away from bone. Remove chicken, debone and shred meat. Return chicken to pot. Add butter. Once butter melts, return to boil. Combine cornstarch with a little milk to soften; add to boiling broth and stir. Slowly add additional milk and return to boil. Reduce heat and simmer just until flavors fuse. Finish recipe to your taste, adding salt or more milk and cornstarch to desired thickness.

Mrs. Sandra Martin
Big Elkin Creek Farm

Stecoah Valley Cultural Arts Center

Soggy Bottom Corn Dumplings with Chili Beans

2 tablespoons extra virgin olive oil
1 onion, chopped or sliced
1 pound ground beef or ground
    turkey
1 (15-ounce) can whole-kernel corn
4 (15-ounce) cans dark red kidney
    beans, liquid reserved
12 ounces salsa
Crushed or chopped garlic to taste
Salt and pepper to taste

1 cup flour, sifted
¾ cup cornmeal, sifted
1 tablespoon baking powder
2 tablespoons sugar
¾ teaspoon salt
1½ teaspoons dried cilantro or 3
    tablespoons fresh
1 cup milk
2 tablespoons butter, melted
1 egg

To make the chili:

Heat olive oil in a 3-quart saucepan. Add onion and cook until clear. Add meat, breaking it up as you add it to the pan. Add corn and kidney beans. Cook until all are done and meat is no longer pink. Add salsa, garlic and salt and pepper to taste. Simmer, covered, 5 minutes.

To make the dumplings:

Place flour, cornmeal, baking powder, sugar, salt and cilantro into a bowl and mix well. In another bowl, mix milk, butter, and egg. Pour wet ingredients into dry ingredients. Stir gently to get dry ingredients wet but do not over stir.

Place spoonfuls of the dumplings onto top of chili. Simmer 10 minutes. Place lid on pan and simmer 10 more minutes. Put any leftover batter into a small, greased cake pan. Bake at 350°, checking for doneness every 5 minutes, until done.

Note: Garlic, salt and pepper are optional as the salsa may spice the chili bean up enough. You can use any kind of beans you desire.

Carol Rose, 1st Place 2006 Yates Mill Cornmeal Cook-off
Historic Yates Mill

Farmhouse Five-Bean Chili

1 pound ground beef
1 large onion, chopped
1 (15-ounce) can butter beans (large limas)
1 (16-ounce) can Bush's Original Baked Beans
1 (15-ounce) can black beans
1 (15-ounce) can light red kidney beans
1 (15-ounce) can dark red kidney beans
2 (14½-ounce) cans diced tomatoes
1 tablespoon chili powder
1 tablespoon red pepper flakes
1 teaspoon onion powder
1 teaspoon garlic powder
1 teaspoon black pepper
Salt if desired

Brown ground beef with onion. Drain fat and discard. Add beans, tomatoes and spices along with ground beef mixture to soup pot or crockpot and simmer for at least 1 hour or at least 3 hours if using a crockpot. Add water if necessary to thin.

1861 Farmhouse Market

Tailgate Chili

This recipe makes enough for a party.

3 pounds ground beef
2 (28-ounce) cans diced tomatoes, undrained
4 cans (16-ounce kidney beans, rinsed and drained
1 pound link sausage, sliced and halved
2 large onions, halved and thinly sliced
2 (8-ounce) cans tomato sauce
⅔ cup barbecue sauce
1½ cups water

½ cup packed brown sugar
5 banana peppers, seeded and sliced
2 tablespoons chili powder
2 teaspoons ground mustard
1 teaspoon dried oregano
1 teaspoon thyme
1 teaspoon sage
½ teaspoon cayenne pepper
½ teaspoon crushed red pepper flakes
2 garlic cloves, minced

In an 8-quart pot, brown ground beef; drain. Add remaining ingredients and bring to a boil. Reduce heat, cover and simmer 1 hour, stirring occasionally. Serve hot. Delicious topped with shredded Cheddar cheese or served over steaming white rice.

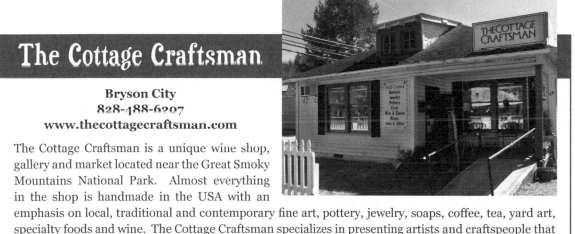

The Cottage Craftsman

Bryson City
828-488-6207
www.thecottagecraftsman.com

The Cottage Craftsman is a unique wine shop, gallery and market located near the Great Smoky Mountains National Park. Almost everything in the shop is handmade in the USA with an emphasis on local, traditional and contemporary fine art, pottery, jewelry, soaps, coffee, tea, yard art, specialty foods and wine. The Cottage Craftsman specializes in presenting artists and craftspeople that live, work and play in the mountains of Western North Carolina and the surrounding region. More than half of the wines are from North Carolina and the Blue Ridge. Most Saturdays from Memorial Day through October, there are free wine tastings featuring chosen wines of the week.

Batty Black and Blue Salad

This is an easy salad and loved by all. The quantity of all items is totally up to you.

Mixed greens
Chopped dates
Red onion, sliced thin
Apples, sliced thin

Crumbled blue cheese
Grilled blackened chicken,
  chopped

Combine all ingredients, toss well, chill and serve.

John and Joann D'Ambra
Old Cider Mill

Tuna Antipasto Salad for Two

1 cup cooked beans (chickpeas, black-
  eyed peas or kidney beans)
1 (5-ounce) can chunk light tuna,
  drained and flaked
½ cup finely diced red bell pepper
½ cup finely chopped red onion
¼ cup chopped fresh parsley, divided

2 teaspoons capers, rinsed
¾ teaspoon finely chopped fresh
  rosemary
4 tablespoons lemon juice, divided
2 tablespoons olive oil, divided
Fresh ground pepper to taste
4 cups mixed salad greens

Combine beans, tuna, bell pepper, onion, parsley, capers, rosemary, 2 tablespoons lemon juice and 1 tablespoon oil in a bowl. Season with pepper. Combine remaining lemon juice and oil in a large bowl. Add salad greens and toss to coat. Divide greens between 2 plates. Top each with tuna mixture.

Linda Whisnant, Old Bridge Cookbook
Old Bridge Preservation Society

Grilled Fig Salad with Prosciutto

24 small fresh figs, halved
2 tablespoons extra virgin olive oil
1½ tablespoons balsamic vinegar
2 tablespoons minced rosemary

Salt and pepper to taste
1 pound arugula, stems discarded
2 cups flat-leaf parsley
½ pound thinly sliced prosciutto

Preheat grill pan or grill. Place half the figs, cut side down, on grill and cook 1 to 2 minutes until lightly charred. In a large bowl add olive oil, vinegar and rosemary. Season with salt and pepper and whisk until blended. Add arugula, parsley and grilled figs and toss with dressing. Place prosciutto slices on plates. Arrange salad on the prosciutto and top with uncooked figs. Drizzle any remaining dressing over top. Serve with Silver Coast Winery Calabash Blush and crusty bread.

Al Gomes
Silver Coast Winery

Mandarin Salad

½ cup slivered almonds
3 tablespoons sugar
½ head leaf lettuce
½ head romaine lettuce

1 cup sliced celery
2 green onions, chopped
1 (11-ounce) can mandarin
     oranges, drained

Dressing:

½ teaspoon salt
Dash pepper
¼ cup oil

1 tablespoon parsley
2 tablespoons sugar
2 tablespoons vinegar

In small saucepan over medium heat, cook almonds and sugar, stirring constantly, until almonds are coated and sugar is dissolved. Watch carefully, they burn easily! Cool and store in airtight container.

Mix dressing ingredients and chill. Tear lettuces into pieces and toss with celery and green onions. Just before serving, pour dressing over salad and top with oranges and almonds.

Creedmoor Music Festival

Caprese Salad

3 tomatoes, sliced ¼–inch thick
1 pound fresh mozzarella, sliced ¼-inch thick
1 bunch fresh basil
Extra virgin olive oil
Salt and pepper

On a large platter, layer alternating slices of tomatoes and mozzarella, adding a basil leaf between each. Drizzle with olive oil and season with salt and pepper, to taste.

Greensboro Science Center

4301 Lawndale Drive
Greensboro
336-288-3769
www.greensboroscience.org

The Greensboro Science Center is a premier family attraction in North Carolina that offers the state's first inland aquarium, a hands-on science museum, an accredited Animal Discovery Zoological Park and a state-of-the-art OmniSphere Dome Theater. The Center is also North Carolina's only dually accredited AZA (Association of Zoos and Aquariums) and AAM (American Alliance of Museums) science attraction – an honor only 14 attractions can claim in the nation.

Green Goddess Salad

Mayonnaise:

4 egg yolks
2 tablespoons Dijon mustard
1½ tablespoons lemon juice

Pinch salt
3 cups canola oil

Whisk yolks, mustard, lemon juice and salt together and then emulsify by slowly adding oil while constantly whisking until mixture reaches desired consistency.

Green Goddess Dressing:

2 cups flat leaf parsley
2 cups watercress or arugula
¼ cup tarragon
2 garlic cloves
4 salt-packed anchovies

3 cups mayonnaise, homemade or
  store bought
Juice of 1 lemon
2 tablespoons champagne vinegar

Purée parsley, watercress, tarragon, garlic and anchovies. Combine with mayonnaise, lemon juice and champagne vinegar. Makes 1 quart.

Salad Mix (per serving):

½ head romaine, torn into pieces
½ avocado, cut into chunks

¼ English cucumber, chopped
Chopped chives and parsley, garnish

Mix 2 tablespoons dressing with each serving of salad mix and garnish with chives and parsley.

Chef Bill Klein
River House Inn

Egg Salad

1 (3-ounce) package cream cheese, softened
¼ cup mayonnaise
½ teaspoon salt
⅛ teaspoon pepper
¼ cup green or sweet red pepper
¼ cup finely chopped celery
¼ cup sweet pickle relish
8 tablespoons minced fresh parsley
8 hard-cooked eggs, chopped

In a bowl, beat cream cheese, mayonnaise, salt and pepper until smooth. Add green pepper, celery, relish, and parsley. Fold in eggs. Refrigerate until ready to serve.

Luann Rivenbark
North Carolina Poultry Jubilee

Ronda's Chicken Salad

1 whole chicken
Mayonnaise or salad dressing
1 cup diced sweet pickles

1 cup diced celery
Salt and pepper to taste
Sweet pickle juice

Boil chicken until done. Remove from stock (save stock to use later). Let chicken cool and then debone and shred the meat. Mix chicken, mayonnaise, pickles, celery, salt and pepper. If salad is too dry, add a small amount of pickle juice to make the consistency you like.

Ronda Rivenbark
North Carolina Poultry Jubilee

Potato Salad

1 cups mayonnaise
1 tablespoon mustard
½ cup heavy cream
¼ cup sugar
1 small onion, grated
3 eggs, boiled and chopped

1 cup chopped celery
½ cup diced green pepper
14 small potatoes, cooked, peeled
  and diced
Salt and pepper to taste
Paprika

Combine mayonnaise, mustard, cream, sugar, onion, eggs, celery and green pepper in large bowl. Add potatoes. Blend carefully, taken care to not mash the potatoes. Add salt and pepper. Sprinkle with paprika. Cool thoroughly before serving.

Apple Slaw

½ cup mayonnaise
2 tablespoons sugar
2 tablespoons salad vinegar
1 large head cabbage

2 chopped apples (use any crisp apple)
½ cup diced celery
½ cup Craisins
½ cup chopped pecans

Mix the first 3 ingredients to make the dressing and set aside. Reserve several large cabbage leaves and shred remaining cabbage. Add the salad dressing to the shredded cabbage, apples, celery, Craisins and pecans. Mix thoroughly and serve in a cabbage leaf-lined bowl.

Bonnie Schmink
The Orchard at Altapass

Sunrise Slaw

¼ teaspoon Cajun seasoning
¼ teaspoon red pepper flakes
¼ teaspoon cumin seed
1 teaspoon sugar or sugar substitute
Zest and juice of 2 limes
¼ cup vegetable oil
1 carrot, cut into fine strips
1 small jicama, cut into fine strips

½ red pepper, cut into fine strips
½ yellow pepper, cut into fine strips
2 cups quartered North Carolina
  strawberries
¼ cup black olives, pitted and sliced
1 red chili pepper, cut into fine dice
½ teaspoon chopped cilantro

Place Cajun seasoning, red pepper flakes, cumin and sugar in a bowl; add lime zest and juice. Whisk in oil. Add remaining ingredients and mix together well. Place in refrigerator to infuse flavors about 1 hour before serving. Serve as side dish or with pan-roasted fish. Makes 4 to 6 servings.

Chef Mark Allison, Johnson & Wales University,
for The Strawberry Project
www.ncmarketready.org/strawberry-project/
Gross Farms

Eastern-Style Slaw

6 medium heads cabbage, finely shredded (about 36 cups)
1½ cups green onion, sliced
1½ quarts mayonnaise or salad dressing
¾ cup sugar
¾ cup vinegar
2 to 4 tablespoons celery seed
2 tablespoons salt to taste

In large bowl, combine cabbage and onion. In small bowl, blend mayonnaise, sugar, vinegar, celery seed and salt. Mix well. Drizzle mayonnaise mixture over cabbage mixture in bowl. Toss lightly to mix well. Refrigerate until serving. Makes 50 servings.

Newport Pig Cooking Contest

Gross Farms

Best Grape Salad

2 pounds green seedless grapes
2 pounds red seedless grapes
8 ounces sour cream
8 ounces cream cheese, softened

½ cup sugar
1 teaspoon vanilla extract
1 cup brown sugar, packed
1 cup crushed pecans

Wash and stem grapes. Set aside. Mix sour cream, cream cheese, sugar and vanilla by hand until blended. Stir grapes into mixture and pour into large serving bowl. Combine brown sugar and crushed pecans. Sprinkle over top of grapes to cover completely.

Sonya Snyder, Town of Cary Parks,
Recreation and Cultural Resources Department employee
Cary Kite Festival

Cary Kite Festival

March

Fred G. Bond Metro Park
Cary
919-469-4100
www.townofcary.org

Join the town of Cary and let imaginations and kites soar at the Cary Kite Festival. The first Kite Festival took flight in Fred G. Bond Metro Park in 1995. Each year Caryites and people from around the state come to see kites rise and descend in the North Carolina blue sky. This family friendly event offers fun contests in a variety of categories for all generations. Awards are given for the highest flying kite, the kite that takes flight the fastest, the smallest kite, largest kite, or the most un-flyable! No matter what the skill level, there is a prize for everyone. On the morning of the Kite Festival, children can make and decorate their own kites in the Kite Making Class. Come Fly with Cary!

Pears Topped with Black Pepper Farmers Cheese

2 large pears, halved and cored
1 teaspoon fresh lemon juice
⅓ cup Buffalo Creek Farm Farmers Goat Cheese Encrusted with Black Pepper,
  crumbled

Brush sides of pears with lemon juice. Place pears on individual dessert plates and sprinkle with goat cheese.

Buffalo Creek Farm and Creamery

Orange Salad

1 (8-ounce) container sour cream
1 (12-ounce) container Cool Whip
2 (3-ounce) boxes orange Jell-O
1 (8.25-ounce) can mandarin oranges, drained and cut up
1 (8-ounce) can crushed pineapple, drained

Mix sour cream, Cool Whip and Jell-O well; add orange and pineapple. Spread in 8- or 9-inch square dish and refrigerate. Cut into squares when set.

Creedmoor Music Festival

Blue Cheese Salad Dressing

1 quart mayonnaise
½ pound blue cheese crumbles
¼ cup finely chopped onion
1 teaspoon dry mustard
1 cup sour cream
1 cup milk

Combine ingredients and store tightly covered in refrigerator. Best if made a day ahead.

Fryemont Inn

Rémoulade Sauce

2 tablespoons fresh lemon juice
3 tablespoons vegetable oil
¼ cup chopped onion
¼ cup chopped green onion
2 tablespoons chopped celery
1 tablespoon chopped garlic
1 tablespoon prepared horseradish
1½ tablespoons Creole mustard
1½ tablespoons yellow mustard
2 tablespoons ketchup
1½ tablespoons chopped parsley
½ teaspoon salt
Dash cayenne pepper
Dash black pepper

Combine all ingredients in food processor and process 30 seconds. Store in tightly covered jar in refrigerator.

Fryemont Inn

Vegetables & Other Side Dishes

Farmer's Casserole

3 cups frozen hash browns
¾ cup shredded Cheddar Cheese
1 cup diced ham, cooked
4 eggs
1 (12-ounce) can evaporated milk

¼ teaspoon pepper
⅛ teaspoon salt
¼ cup chopped green onion
  (optional)

Grease 2-quart square baking dish. Arrange potatoes in bottom of dish. Sprinkle cheese, ham and green onion over potatoes. In medium mixing bowl combine eggs, milk, pepper and salt. Pour egg mixture over potatoes. Bake uncovered at 350° for 40 to 45 minutes or until center is set. Let stand 5 minutes before serving.

The Inn at Elk River

The Inn at Elk River

Havarti Chive Mashed Potatoes

2½ pounds potatoes
1 tablespoon salt
Pepper to taste
1 stick (4-ounces) butter

8 slices Havarti cheese, cut into
  pieces
2 tablespoons fresh or dried chives

Prepare mashed potatoes as usual. Season with salt and pepper. Add butter and cheese, stirring until melted. Stir in chives.

Buttermilk can be used to thin out potatoes if desired. These taste so good you do not need to serve gravy.

Jean Smith, Old Bridge Cookbook
Old Bridge Preservation Society

Apple-Sweet Potato Baked Casserole

5 medium-size tart apples
6 medium sweet potatoes, cooked
  whole with skins left on
½ cup brown sugar, honey or maple
  syrup

½ cup chopped pecans or walnuts
1 teaspoon salt
1 teaspoon cinnamon
¼ teaspoon nutmeg
½ teaspoon allspice

Core unpeeled apples and cut into rings. Peel potatoes and cut into lengthwise slices about ½-inch thick. Alternate layers of potatoes, apples, sugar, nuts and seasonings in a greased casserole dish. Cover and bake in 325° oven about 45 minutes.

Brushy Mountain Ruritan Club
Brushy Mountain Apple Festival

Roasted Root Veggies with Mead

3 parsnips
3 carrots
2 sweet potatoes
1 butternut squash, peeled and seeded
2 tablespoon of olive oil, divided
2 cups Starrlight Mead Semi-sweet Traditional Mead
2 peeled whole garlic cloves
Dash of sea salt and fresh ground pepper to taste

Dice all vegetables except garlic to an even size, roughly ¼ inch. In a large bowl combine 1 tablespoon olive oil, mead, diced veggies and garlic. Cover and refrigerate at least 1 hour.

Preheat oven to 375°. Remove marinated veggies and arrange evenly on a baking sheet. Drizzle remaining olive oil over veggies and add salt and pepper to taste. Bake 30 minutes. Serve with chilled mead and enjoy!

Charles Pace, employee
Starrlight Mead

Sweet Potato Casserole

3 cups cooked sweet potatoes
1 cup sugar
3 eggs
½ cup milk

Dash of salt
1 teaspoon vanilla
½ stick butter, melted

Topping:

1 cup brown sugar
¼ cup flour

½ cup butter, softened
¾ cup chopped pecans

Combine casserole ingredients and beat with mixer until smooth. Place in 2-quart casserole. Mix topping ingredients together and spread over casserole. Bake uncovered 30 minutes at 350°.

Evelyn McNeill Waddell
Columbus County Community Farmers Market

Columbus County Community Farmers Market

COLUMBUS COUNTY
COMMUNITY

FARMERS
MARKET

Established 1998

132 Government Complex Road
Whiteville
910-840-6743
www.columbuscountyfarmersmarket.com

Open Tuesdays and Saturdays 7am to 1pm
during May through December

The Columbus County Farmers Community Market—with an emphasis on "community"—was established in 1998 in a downtown Whiteville parking lot by a small group of growers, most of whom had transitioned from tobacco to fruits and vegetables. Today, the Market is a great source of locally grow, farm fresh fruits, vegetables, herbs, honey, eggs, preserves, baked goods, crafts and more. Special events are held each month to promote better nutrition, health and wellness, and physical activity.

Honey Almond Sweet Potatoes

1 cup cooked sweet potatoes, sliced
¼ cup honey
¼ cup orange marmalade
3 tablespoons water

1 teaspoon salt
⅓ cup butter
¼ cup blanched slivered almonds

Place sliced sweet potatoes in a single player in greased baking dish. Combine honey, marmalade, water and salt. Bring to boil, reduce heat, and simmer 5 minutes. Pour over potatoes. Melt butter in small frying pan, add almonds and toast over low heat until golden brown. Sprinkle over potatoes, bake at 325° for 30 minutes or until glazed, basting occasionally.

Kernersville Honeybee Festival

Kernersville Honeybee Festival

August

Fourth of July Park
Kernersville
336-996-3062
www.kvhoneybee.com

In 1973, Brady Mullinax began his effort to distinguish the honeybee as the state insect. He took then State Honey Queen, Pat Dollarhite, to Raleigh. As she drizzled honey from a honey bear on their biscuits, she said "Who wouldn't vote in favor of the Honeybee Bill?" The bill was passed and the honeybee became North Carolina's official state insect. In the summer of 1975, Kernersville citizens brought up the idea of a festival celebrating Brady's accomplishments. It was fitting that the festival be called the Kernersville Honeybee Festival.

Today, the Kernersville Honeybee Festival consists of over 85+ vendors and attracts well over 10,000 spectators. There are live craft demonstrations, scrumptious food, games, arts and crafts, music, a kid's play area and of course, HONEY! Brady's apprentice, Craig Cagle, can be found selling his homemade honey in Brady's original booth space in the park.

Sautéed Swiss Chard with Spring Onions and Green Garlic

2 to 3 spring onions, whites and tops chopped
1 bunch Swiss chard, stems diced and leaves rough chopped
1 tablespoon olive oil
1 minced green garlic bulb or to taste
Grated Parmesan-style Buffalo Creek Farm Rock House Goat Cheese

Sauté onions and chard stems in olive oil until soft. Add garlic and sauté 1 minute more. Add Swiss chard leaves and sauté until wilted and tender, approximately 3 to 5 minutes. Top with grated goat cheese to taste.

Recipe courtesy of Mother Holtz Farm
Buffalo Creek Farm and Creamery

Swiss Chard Goat Cheese Casserole

1 bunch Swiss chard or spinach, stems diced and leaves rough chopped
1 Buffalo Creek Farm pastured egg
1 cup milk
⅓ cup melted butter
½ cup toasted breadcrumbs, divided
Dash cayenne pepper (omit if using Red Pepper Chevre)
1 teaspoon anchovy paste or salt to taste
8 ounces fresh Buffalo Creek Farm Plain or Red Pepper Chevre, room
    temperature

Cook chard in ½ cup salted water until wilted. Drain and squeeze out excess water. Blend in food processor 15 to 20 seconds. Combine egg, milk, butter, ¼ cup breadcrumbs, cayenne pepper, anchovy paste and chevre. Stir in chard. Place in greased 1-quart casserole and top with remaining breadcrumbs. Bake in 350° oven 35 to 40 minutes.

Recipe courtesy of Mother Holtz Farm
Buffalo Creek Farm and Creamery

Braised Red Cabbage

1 tablespoon olive oil
3 large onions, thinly sliced (about 2
   pounds)
¼ teaspoon ground cinnamon
¼ teaspoon ground cloves
¼ teaspoon ground cumin

1 small red cabbage, thinly sliced
   (about 1 pound)
¼ cup apple cider
¼ cup brown sugar
¼ cup red wine vinegar

In a large pot heat olive oil over medium-high heat and sauté onions until soft. Add cinnamon, cloves and cumin and cook 30 seconds. Mix in cabbage and sauté 5 minutes until wilted. Add cider, sugar and vinegar. Cover and braise over low heat until cabbage is tender, about 20 minutes. Serve warm.

Creedmoor Music Festival

Stuffed Cabbage Rolls

⅔ cup water
⅓ cup uncooked white rice
8 cabbage leaves
1 pound lean ground beef
¼ cup chopped onion

1 egg, lightly beaten
1 teaspoon salt
¼ teaspoon ground black pepper
1 (10¾-ounce) can condensed tomato
   soup

In a medium saucepan, bring water to a boil. Add rice and stir. Reduce heat, cover and simmer 20 minutes.

Bring a large, wide saucepan of lightly salted water to a boil. Add cabbage leaves and cook 2 to 4 minutes or until softened; drain.

In a medium mixing bowl, combine ground beef, 1 cup cooked rice, onion, egg, salt and pepper and 2 tablespoons tomato soup. Mix thoroughly. Divide beef mixture evenly among the cabbage leaves. Roll and secure them with toothpicks or string. Place the cabbage rolls in a large skillet over medium heat and pour the remaining tomato soup over the top. Cover and bring to a boil. Reduce heat to low and simmer about 40 minutes, stirring and basting with the liquid often.

Nancy Hawley
MUMFEST, New Bern

Grilled Asparagus Wrapped with Prosciutto

16 asparagus spears, base ends removed
8 thin slices prosciutto
Olive oil
Lemon wedges

Wrap two asparagus spears with a slice of prosciutto, making 8 bundles total. Brush with olive oil and grill on high 1 to 2 minutes each side. Squeeze fresh lemon juice on top at serving. Serve with Adagio Vineyards Vivace

Adagio Vineyards

Adagio Vineyards

139 Benge Drive
Elkin
336-258-2333
www.adagiovineyards.com

Located in the foothills of the Blue Ridge Mountains, Adagio Vineyards is where all five senses are met with extraordinary elegance. Adagio is a musical term which means performed slowly and passionately, two descriptors which apply to the growing and making of wine. The vineyard and winery are named after Adagio because it represents the owner's passions for classical music and wine. The tasting room reflects these passions, featuring fine wines and showcasing hand crafted violins and violin making. Here guests can experience fine wine, music, and explore the process of creating handmade violins, a true artisan process. There are 6 acres of grapes, growing two red varietals, Merlot and Arandell. Arandell is a French American hybrid grape which produces a deeply colored wine with intense flavor. Chardonnay and Traminette are the white varietals. Traminette is also a French American hybrid which closely resembles a guwurtztraminer, producing a bright wine with a floral nose.

Grilled Mushrooms with Prosciutto & Melted Cheese

6 medium mushrooms (portabello are great)

5 tablespoons olive oil

1 tablespoons garlic powder

2 tablespoons black pepper

6 slices prosciutto (if not available, lean pastrami)

½ pound thinly sliced mozzarella cheese

3 tablespoons chopped fresh parsley

Remove mushroom caps, and sauté stems in butter until tender. Wipe caps with a damp towel. Mix olive oil, garlic powder and pepper and brush mushrooms with mixture. Grill or broil, cap side facing heat, 4 to 5 minutes or until slightly brown. Turn and cook until tender. Place 1 layer prosciutto in center of cap. Add sautéed chopped stems and cover with cheese. Broil 1 minute to melt cheese. Arrange on plate and sprinkle with parsley. Serve with Silver Coast Winery Touriga.

Al Gomes
Silver Coast Winery

Silver Coast Winery

6680 Barbeque Road NW
Ocean Isle Beach
910-287-2800
www.facebook.com/SilverCoastWinery

Silver Coast Winery is an active wine making facility, opened in 2002 by Maryann and her husband Dr. "Bud" Azzato. Silver Coast wines are modeled after traditional, European styles. All wines are produced in-house by Award Winning Winemaker Dana Keeler, using regionally grown grapes. Guests are welcome to visit the Ocean Isle Beach location for wine tastings and tours of the full production facility. During visits they can relax and enjoy a wine tasting with one of the friendly staff, browse the gift shops, and the eclectic art gallery featuring local artists. The Winery is located in beautiful woodland setting, just minutes away from the beach, specializing in wedding ceremonies, receptions and rehearsal dinners from small intimate gatherings to large banquets. Check their website and Facebook Page for hours and special events.

Baked Mushrooms

1 pound fresh mushrooms, quartered
1 onion, diced
1 clove garlic, chopped
1 green bell pepper, diced
½ teaspoon Italian seasoning
¼ teaspoon seasoning salt
1 dash pepper
2 tablespoons chopped fresh parsley
2 tablespoons water
4 tablespoons melted butter

Preheat oven to 350°. In a 9x13-inch casserole dish combine mushrooms, onion, garlic, green pepper, Italian seasoning, seasoning salt, pepper and parsley. Pour water and butter over mixture and cover. Bake 40 to 45 minutes; serve warm.

Silver Coast Winery Tasting Room

There is also a Tasting Room in downtown Southport where guests can partake in the relaxed atmosphere and enjoy a wine or craft beer tasting. Browse the shop for gifts and wonderful art.

Local Apple-Squash Bake

1 local winter squash (acorn, butternut, buttercup, delicata)
3 or 4 local apples
Maple syrup to taste
½ teaspoon cinnamon
½ cup chopped walnuts
Fresh cranberries
½ cup apple cider

Preheat oven to 375°. Peel, core and cube squash and apples. Place squash in baking dish with a good glug of maple syrup, cinnamon, walnuts, a sprinkling of cranberries and apple cider. Bake until squash is almost fork tender, about 10 minutes. Add apples and bake until apples are tender, about another 10-15 minutes. Serve and enjoy!

Appalachian Sustainable Agriculture Project

Billy Graham Library Home Place

Zucchini Cakes

2½ cups grated zucchini
1 egg, beaten
2 tablespoons butter, melted
½ cup fine, dry breadcrumbs
½ cup panko crumbs

¼ cup minced onion
1 tablespoon Old Bay seasoning
¼ cup all-purpose flour
½ cup vegetable or peanut oil

In a large bowl, combine zucchini, egg and butter. Stir in both kinds of crumbs, onion and Old Bay. Shape into patties and dredge in flour. Refrigerate 15 minutes. Heat oil in medium skillet and fry patties until crisp and golden brown on both sides. Serve with Rémoulade Sauce.

Fryemont Inn

The Fryemont Inn

245 Fryemont Street
Bryson City
800-845-4879 • 828-488-2159
www.fryemontinn.com

Built in 1923 and listed on the National Register of Historic Places, the Fryemont Inn includes a beautiful poplar bark covered historic lodge with two enormous stone fireplaces, eight luxury fireplace suites and a two bedroom cabin. All rates (except winter rates) include breakfast and dinner. The Fryemont Inn dining room is famous for homemade everything! Soups, salad dressings, desserts and sides are made fresh daily. Dinner is a four course meal which features a choice of local rainbow trout, braised lamb shanks, prime rib, and many other delicious entrees. At breakfast guests can choose eggs cooked to order, omelets, pancakes, French toast, or they can try the wonderful biscuits with sausage gravy or salty country ham. Cocktails, wine and hand crafted local beers are available in the cozy fireside bar. The swimming pool, open in the summer months, is nestled in a grove of poplar and dogwood trees.

FRYEMONT INN
Since 1923

Sorghum Glazed Carrots

½ cup unsalted butter
2 pounds baby carrots, peeled
½ cup sorghum syrup
½ cup fresh orange juice
6 tablespoons bourbon
Kosher salt and freshly ground black pepper

 Melt butter in a large skillet over medium heat. Add carrots and sauté until beginning to soften, about 10 minutes. Add sorghum. Cook 2 minutes. Remove from heat; stir in orange juice and bourbon. Return to stove and reduce heat to medium-low. Cover skillet and cook, stirring occasionally, until carrots are fork tender, 5 to 7 minutes. Uncover and cook until liquid has been reduced to a syrupy consistency and carrots are nicely glazed, about 6 minutes. Season to taste with salt and pepper.

Tour De Food
Recipe Courtesy of Mimosa Grill,
a stop on Tour De Food in Charlotte
704-375-9715 • www.harpersgroup.com

Glazed Carrots

2 tablespoons butter or margarine
¼ cup packed brown sugar
1 tablespoon water
3 cups cooked carrots, cut in strips or rounds

Blend butter, sugar and water in heavy fry pan over low heat. Add carrots. Cook over low heat 7 to 10 minutes, turning carrots to evenly coat in syrup. Keep heat low to prevent scorching.

Mill Spring Farm Store

Southern Fried Okra

6 cups okra, sliced about ½ inch
  thick
½ cup cooking oil, divided

¾ cup House Autry Corn Meal
½ cup all-purpose flour
Salt and black pepper to taste

Rinse okra in colander and let drain. Heat ¼ cup oil in a cast-iron or regular skillet over medium-high heat. Combine cornmeal, flour, salt and pepper in a paper bag or medium-size bowl. Toss okra to coat evenly. Allow okra to set a few minutes for cornmeal to stick well. Shake off excess batter with spoon when transferring to skillet. Cook in batches, frying on 1 side until lightly browned, then begin to stir-fry, moving okra around and scraping bottom of pan to avoid burning. When done frying, transfer to paper towels to drain and sprinkle with salt to taste. Prepare next batch, adding additional oil to pan as needed between batches. Serve hot.

Johnston County Visitors Bureau

Flash Fried Onions

1 small onion
½ cup self-rising flour
½ cup cornmeal

1 egg, beaten
Oil for frying
Salt for sprinkling

Cut onion into thin slices and separate into rings. Mix flour and cornmeal. Dredge rings in egg and then in flour. Deep-fry until golden. Drain on paper towels and sprinkle with salt.

Onion Casserole

2 pounds onions, chopped large
1 stick butter

2 cups cracker crumbs
Salt and pepper to taste

Sauté onions in butter until tender. Mix cracker crumbs and salt and pepper with sautéed onions and pour into 9x9-inch casserole. Bake uncovered at 350° until it begins to brown.

Evelyn McNeill Waddell
Columbus County Community Farmers Market

Broccoli Casserole

5 tablespoons butter, divided
1 onion, chopped
2 (10-ounce) packages chopped frozen broccoli, thawed
1 (10¾-ounce) can condensed cream of mushroom soup
1 cup shredded sharp Cheddar cheese
1 cup mayonnaise
2 eggs, beaten
½ teaspoon garlic salt
¼ teaspoon ground black pepper
½ teaspoon seasoned salt
1½ teaspoons lemon juice
12 buttery round crackers, crushed fine

Preheat oven to 350°. Melt 3 tablespoons butter in medium skillet over medium-high heat. Sauté onion until golden. In a 2-quart casserole dish, mix onion with remaining ingredients except the crackers and 2 tablespoons butter. Sprinkle crushed crackers over top and dot with remaining butter. Bake uncovered 45 minutes until heated through and browned on top.

Creedmoor Music Festival

Broccoli-Corn Casserole

Passed down from Mother Graham, Morrow Coffey Graham, mother of Billy.

1 (10-ounce) package frozen broccoli, florets or spears
1 (15.5-ounce) can cream-style corn
2 eggs
Seasoned breadcrumbs
Butter

Preheat oven to 350°. Cook broccoli in small amount of lightly salted water until soft enough to mash, perhaps 15 minutes or so. Drain, then mash. Add corn, mix well, then add eggs. Mix all thoroughly, pour into buttered casserole dish. Sprinkle top with seasoned crumbs, dot with butter. Place in preheated oven. Bake until casserole begins cooking around the edges. Reduce heat to 300° and cook slowly, maybe 35 or 40 minutes longer.

Note from Mother Graham: I buy Pepperidge Farm seasoned crumbs or stuffing. They give a good flavor, and one package will do a number of casseroles if stored in glass jar or tightly sealed container. Usually the crumbs in bottom of the bag are nicer for topping or else the larger ones may be crushed with a rolling pin.

Billy Graham Library

Corn Pudding

As seen in Cookin' up a Storm *by Jane Lee Rankin of Apple Hill Farm.*

4 eggs	½ teaspoon salt
1 cup cream	1 pound frozen corn, thawed
¼ cup sugar	4 tablespoons unsalted butter

Butter a 2-quart casserole dish. In a large bowl, beat the eggs, cream, sugar and salt together. Add corn and stir to combine. Pour corn mixture into casserole dish. Slice butter and arrange on top of corn mixture. Bake at 350° for 1 hour or until top is golden brown and casserole is set. Makes 8 servings.

Apple Hill Farm

Baked Corn Pudding

4 tablespoons butter, melted ¾ cup sugar
¾ cup milk 2 cups corn
2 tablespoons flour ½ teaspoon salt
2 eggs Dash black pepper

Mix all ingredients together and pour into a buttered baking dish. Bake at 375° for 30 to 40 minutes. Shake the dish to make sure the center is set.

Betty Lou Watson
Creedmoor Music Festival

Fried Corn

2 tablespoons bacon grease 1 tablespoon butter
2 cups corn kernels, frozen Sugar to taste
1 tablespoon flour Salt and pepper to taste

Put bacon grease and corn in a frying pan and cook the water out. Add flour when water is cooked out. Brown corn, watching it closely, and then mix in a little water. Add butter, sugar, salt and pepper. Simmer, stirring occasionally.

Ricky Watson
Creedmoor Music Festival

Bacon & Swiss Casserole

1½ (8-ounce) packages Pillsbury Butter Crescent Rolls
1 (7-ounce) package thickly sliced Swiss cheese
14 eggs, well beaten
2 (5-ounce) cans evaporated milk
Lawry's seasoned salt to taste
Pepper to taste
Cooked bacon slices to cover top, about 16 slices

Preheat oven to 350°. Separate and press crescent dough into bottom and 1 inch up the sides of a lightly greased 11x15-inch glass baking dish. Place cheese slices over dough. In a bowl, combine eggs, evaporated milk and salt and pepper. Pour mixture over cheese. Place bacon strips on top to completely cover. Cover loosely with foil and bake 45 minutes. Remove foil and bake an additional 15 minutes or until firm.

The Sunset Inn

The Sunset Inn

**9 North Shore Drive E
Sunset Beach
888-575-1001
www.thesunsetinn.net**

The Sunset Inn opened its doors to the beauty of the saltwater marsh and island life in June 2000. The honey-colored wood floors in the entrance and living area shine softly in the light that filters through the large windows. The Inn is not a typical B&B; it is larger with 14 rooms but still has a cozy atmosphere that makes folks feel right at home. An expanded continental breakfast is served each morning , and guests may choose to have their morning meal in the breakfast room or in the privacy of their own room. Each room has a different theme and décor with a king-size bed, wet bar, refrigerator, love seat and private screened porch with rockers. The four grand rooms each have a jetted tub plus a larger corner porch with rockers and porch swings, robes and IPod docks. Come experience the quiet comfort.

Vegetable Quiche

1 baked pie crust
1 cup sliced vegetables (asparagus, squash or okra)
1½ cups grated Italian or Mexican blend cheese

4 eggs
1 cup milk
3 green onions, chopped
Salt and pepper
1 sliced tomato

Place vegetables in bottom of pie crust. Top with cheese. Beat together eggs, milk and green onions. Salt and pepper to taste. Pour egg mixture on top of cheese, submerging cheese. Top with tomato slices. Bake at 350° for 45 minutes to 1 hour. Test with toothpick.

Old Mill of Guilford

Varn Rice

¼ stick butter
1 cup long grain rice (not instant)
1 (10.5-ounce) French onion soup

1 (10.5-ounce) can beef consommé soup

Melt butter in an ovenproof glass dish while oven is preheating to 350°. Add rice and soups. Bake until liquid is gone, about 40 minutes.

Margaret R. Varn
Catawba Science Center

Farro Risotto

8 cups chicken stock
Salt and freshly ground pepper to taste
2 tablespoons extra virgin olive oil
¼ pound butter
1 pound leeks, white part only, rinsed
   and finely chopped
2 garlic cloves, minced

2 cups farro, uncooked
1 cup white wine
½ cup chopped fresh parsley and thyme
½ cup Parmesan cheese
2 tablespoons fresh lemon juice
1 cup heavy cream

Bring stock to a simmer in a saucepan. Season well and turn heat to low. Heat oil and butter over medium heat in a large pan and add leeks. Cook, stirring, until they begin to soften, about 3 minutes. Add a generous pinch of salt and the garlic. Cook 3 minutes. Add farro and cook 5 minutes. Stir in wine and cook over medium heat, stirring constantly. The wine should bubble, but not too quickly. You want some of the flavor to cook into the farro before it evaporates. When the wine has just about evaporated, stir in a ladleful or 2 of the simmering stock, about ½ cup or enough to just cover the rice. The stock should bubble slowly (adjust heat accordingly). Cook, stirring often, until liquid is just about absorbed. Add another ladleful or 2 of stock and continue to cook in this fashion, not too fast and not too slow, stirring often and adding more stock when the rice is almost dry, for 15 minutes.

Add more stock to cover farro and continue to cook, adding more stock as necessary and stirring often, for another 20 minutes or until the farro is cooked through but al dente. If it is still hard in the middle, you need to continue adding stock and stirring another 20 minutes or so. Add in cream and cook until nice and creamy. Stir in herbs and fresh pepper (be generous). Add the Parmesan and lemon juice, stir together and remove from heat. The risotto should be creamy; if it isn't, add a little more stock. Stir once, taste and adjust seasonings, and serve.

Tour De Food
Recipe Courtesy of Mimosa Grill,
a stop on Tour De Food in Charlotte
704-375-9715 • www.harpersgroup.com
336-406-6294 www.tourdefood.net

Tour De Food

Eat · Drink · Walk

Brown Rice and Black Bean Casserole

⅓ cup brown rice
1 cup vegetable broth
1 tablespoon olive oil
⅓ cup diced onion
1 medium zucchini, thinly sliced
½ cup sliced mushrooms
½ teaspoon cumin

Salt and pepper to taste
1 (15-ounce) can black beans, drained
1 (4-ounce) can diced green chile peppers, drained
⅓ cup shredded carrots
2 cups shredded Swiss cheese, divided

Combine rice and vegetable broth in a pot; bring to a boil. Reduce heat to low, cover, and simmer 45 minutes, or until rice is tender. Preheat oven to 350°. Spray 9x13-inch baking dish with non-stick cooking spray. Heat olive oil in a skillet over medium heat, and sauté onion until tender. Add zucchini, mushrooms, cumin, salt and pepper. Cook and stir until zucchini is lightly browned. In large bowl, mix cooked rice, onion, zucchini, mushrooms, beans, chiles, carrots, and 1 cup Swiss cheese. Spread mixture into baking dish, and sprinkle with remaining cheese. Cover loosely with foil and bake 30 minutes. Uncover, and continue baking 10 minutes, or until bubbly and lightly browned.

Baked Cheese Grits Casserole

1 cup grits
1 pound sausage or 12 sausage
    patties
12 eggs
1 (5-ounce) can evaporated milk

1 box Jiffy corn muffin mix
1 (8-ounce) package cream cheese,
    softened
8 cups shredded cheese
Salt and pepper to taste

Cook grits in 4 cups water. Preheat oven to 350°. Brown sausage and crumble. In a large bowl, beat eggs. Whisk in milk and corn muffin mix. Add cream cheese, shredded cheese and sausage to cooked grits. Blend well and stir into egg mixture. Blend well and pour into 11x15-inch glass baking dish that has been sprayed with nonstick spray. Bake 1 hour until a knife inserted in center comes out clean. Cover loosely with foil after about 45 minutes if top is getting too brown.

The Sunset Inn

Cheese Grits Soufflé

1 cup Old Mill of Guilford grits,
    white or yellow
2 cups milk
2 cups water
3 tablespoons butter
1½ cups shredded cheese

½ cup shredded Parmesan cheese
½ teaspoon pepper
Splash each Worcestershire sauce
    and Tabasco
4 eggs, separated

Prepare grits according to directions in bag. When grits are cooked, add cheeses, pepper, Worcestershire sauce and Tabasco. Beat egg yolks and stir into grits. Whip egg whites and fold into grits. Pour into greased baking dish. Bake at 350° for 30 minutes or until puffed and lightly brown.

Old Mill of Guilford

Annie Laura's Grits Casserole

1 pound ground sausage, cooked and drained
2 cups milk
4 eggs
4 cups cooked Old Mill of Guilford grits, white or yellow
12 ounces shredded sharp Cheddar cheese

Crumble sausage on bottom of 9x13-inch baking dish. In large bowl, combine milk and eggs. Add cooked grits and cheese. Blend well and pour over sausage. Bake in 350° oven 1 hour.

Note: You may top with ½ pound shrimp and/or fresh sliced tomatoes.

Old Mill of Guilford

Batty Baked Apples

6 apples, sweet or tart
10 ounces Colby, Jack or Swiss cheese, grated
½ cup brown sugar
½ cup raisins
½ cup sliced almonds

Core apples and spoon out centers. Combine cheese, sugar and raisins and mix well. Spoon into hollowed apples and top with almonds. Bake uncovered at 375° for 45 minutes.

John and Joann D'Ambra
Old Cider Mill

Baked Pineapple

½ cup butter
1 cup white sugar
4 eggs
1 pinch ground cinnamon

1 pinch ground nutmeg
5 slices white bread, torn
1 (20-ounce) can crushed pineapple
   with juice

Preheat oven to 350°). Grease medium-sized casserole dish. In a mixing bowl, cream together butter and sugar. Beat in eggs one at a time. Stir in cinnamon and nutmeg. Add bread and crushed pineapple; toss evenly to coat. Pour mixture into baking dish. Bake 60 minutes.

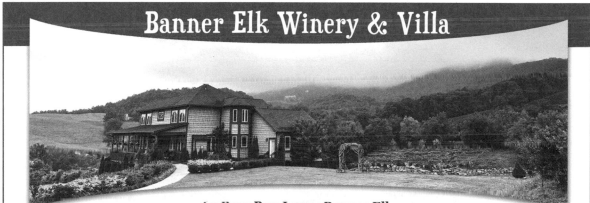

Pickled Baby Bat

1 baby black bat
1 Mason jar with tight seal

Catch bat in Mason jar in the back hills of Bat Cave under a full moon. This recipe is fat free, low in carbs, tastes like chicken and improves night vision. Guaranteed to blow your skirt up or knock your draws down.

WARNING: This recipe may cause blood loss. Serve with your favorite road kill, corn bread and mountain moonshine!!! (This is ONLY a joke, don't even consider making or eating it.)

John and Joann D'Ambra
Old Cider Mill

Hickory Nut Gap Farm

Meat & Seafood

Varn Chicken

1 cup oil
1 egg
2 cups vinegar
2 tablespoons poultry seasoning

2 teaspoons salt
1 teaspoon pepper
1 to 3 small chickens

Beat oil and egg. Add vinegar and mix well. Add poultry seasoning, salt and pepper and mix well. Clean chickens, place them into the marinade and refrigerate overnight. Cook on a charcoal grill.

Margaret R. Varn
Catawba Science Center

Sesame Chicken

1 pound boneless skinless chicken
  breasts
⅓ cup teriyaki sauce
2 teaspoons cornstarch
1 tablespoon peanut or vegetable oil

2 cloves garlic, minced
2 large green onions, cut into ½-inch
  slices
1 tablespoon toasted sesame seeds
1 teaspoon dark sesame oil

Cut chicken into 1-inch pieces; toss with teriyaki sauce in small bowl. Marinate at room temperature 15 minutes or cover and refrigerate up to 2 hours. Drain chicken and reserve marinade. Blend reserved marinade into cornstarch until smooth. Heat wok or large skillet over medium-high heat. Add peanut oil; heat until hot. Add chicken and garlic; stir-fry 3 minutes or until chicken is no longer pink. Stir marinade mixture; add to wok along with onions and sesame seeds. Stir-fry 30 seconds or until sauce boils and thickens. Stir in sesame oil.

Luanne Johnson
North Carolina Poultry Jubilee

Citrus Roasted Chicken

One whole chicken is truly 3 meals in one!

1 (4- to 6-pound) chicken	Olive oil
1 lemon	Salt and pepper
½ onion, chopped	1 teaspoon dried rosemary
3 sprigs fresh rosemary	1 teaspoon oregano

Preheat oven to 400°. Rinse chicken inside and out. Cut lemon into 6 pieces and squeeze juice inside chicken cavity. Insert onion and rosemary sprigs. Lightly rub chicken with olive oil, season with salt, pepper, dried rosemary and oregano. Bake 10 minutes uncovered to seal in juices. Reduce temperature to 325°, cover with aluminum foil and cook an additional 2 hours until done. Let chicken stand at least 10 minutes before carving. Pick the carcass clean and use the pieces of chicken to top a salad.

For Stock:

Chicken carcass	3 stalks celery, rough chop
6 to 8 cups water	2 carrots, rough chop
1 cup chopped onion	

Place carcass in a large stockpot or crockpot and cover with water. Add onion, celery and carrots. Bring to a boil. Reduce heat, cover and simmer 8-plus hours.

Hickory Nut Gap Farm

Drunk-on-Muscadine Chicken

Muscadine grapes are renowned for their healthy benefits, containing the most antioxidants of any other grape. This recipe uses wine from Lu Mil Vineyard.

1 chicken (about 5 pounds), cut into 8 pieces
1 teaspoon salt
½ teaspoon black pepper
2 tablespoon olive or grapeseed oil
1 large sweet onion, thinly sliced
2 garlic cloves, minced
2 tablespoons Dijon mustard

1 cup Lu Mil's Old Cumberland white wine
3 cups chicken broth
2 tablespoons fresh tarragon, chopped
¼ cup chopped parsley, divided
2 tablespoons flour
2 tablespoons water
2 tablespoons unsalted butter

Sprinkle salt and pepper evenly over chicken pieces. In a large saucepan, heat oil over medium-high heat. Brown chicken pieces on all sides, making sure not to crowd pan. Transfer to a platter. Add onion slices to pan and cook, stirring frequently, 5 minutes. Add garlic and mustard; stir 30 more seconds. Deglaze pan by pouring in wine and scraping browned bits off bottom. Return chicken pieces to pan and add chicken broth, tarragon, and half of parsley. Bring to boil, reduce heat and cover pan. Cook 30 minutes or until juices from chicken run clear. Transfer chicken to platter and sprinkle with remaining parsley. Whisk flour and water in small bowl and stir into sauce left in pan. Bring sauce to a simmer and cook until desired thickness (several minutes). Stir in butter and season with additional salt and pepper if necessary. Serve with chicken.

Whisking Apprentice School for Home Cooks, Fayetteville
Lu Mil Vineyard

Steamed Chicken Breast with Garden Vegetables & New Potatoes

1½ pounds small new potatoes or small red potatoes
2 tablespoons olive oil
Kosher salt and fresh cracked black pepper to taste
4 (5- to 7-ounce) boneless, skinless chicken breasts
1 medium or large carrot, washed and peeled
1 medium or large zucchini, washed
8 ounces white or button mushrooms, very thinly sliced
2 to 3 ounces fresh baby spinach
1 fresh shallot, peeled and thinly sliced
1 large garlic clove, minced
1 to 2 tablespoons chopped fresh basil
4 tablespoons unsalted butter, margarine or vegan butter
4 tablespoons dry white wine, such as Chardonnay or Pinot Grigio
4 sheets parchment paper

Preheat oven to 350°. Wash and dry potatoes, place in a bowl and coat with olive oil. Sprinkle with a little salt and pepper, and place on cookie sheet. Bake 25 to 35 minutes or until potatoes are cooked through. While potatoes are baking, assemble the chicken and vegetables. Rinse chicken breasts under cold water and pat dry with paper towels. Sprinkle with a little salt and pepper, and hold in refrigerator. Using a vegetable peeler, cut long strips of the carrot and zucchini. Gather remaining ingredients and assemble packets in this order: Fold parchment paper in half, then open. Using the middle crease as your guide, place one quarter of the spinach in a pile in the middle on 1 side of the crease. On top of the spinach, place one quarter of the mushrooms, then one quarter of the zucchini, one quarter of the carrots, one quarter of the shallots, one quarter of the garlic and one quarter of the basil. Lay 1 chicken breast on top of the vegetables and place 1 tablespoon butter on top of chicken. Sprinkle 1 tablespoon white wine over chicken. Fold parchment paper over top of chicken and vegetables. To seal the package, begin on 1 corner and crimp the paper tightly up and towards the food, working your way around, finishing at the other side. Chicken and vegetables should be completely sealed in a half moon or semi-circular shape. Finish the remaining 3 packages and place them on a cookie sheet and bake 25 to 30 minutes. The paper packages will puff up nicely if properly sealed. Remove from oven and serve on a plate with potatoes on the side. Just be aware that the released steam will be very hot. Makes 4 servings.

Chef Denise Gordon
TheatreNOW

Stuffed Chicken Breast with Sage Mead

6 boneless skinless chicken breasts, pounded ¼ inch thick
1 bottle Starrlight Mead Herb Infused Sage Mead, divided
Sea salt and black pepper to taste
8 slices (½-pound) applewood smoked bacon
1 (10-ounce) package frozen chopped spinach, thawed and squeezed dry
1 cup crumbled blue cheese

Place chicken breasts and 1 cup mead in zip-close bag. Marinate 3 hours in refrigerator. Remove from marinade and set aside on a large platter. Sprinkle evenly with salt and pepper. Arrange bacon in skillet and cook on medium heat, turning until done. Set aside on paper towels. Drain hot bacon fat into cup and return 2 tablespoons to skillet. Set aside.

Preheat oven to 350°. In a medium bowl, stir together spinach and blue cheese. Crumble in bacon and stir to distribute. Lay chicken breasts out on a clean surface and distribute spinach mixture evenly on centers. Fold chicken over filling and secure with toothpicks. Heat skillet with bacon fat over medium-high heat. Quickly brown each piece of chicken on top and bottom. Remove to a lightly greased baking dish and cover with a lid or aluminum foil. Bake 30 minutes until chicken juices run clear and filling is hot. Brush a little mead on the breasts every 10 minutes to keep the outside moist. Enjoy with remaining bottle of mead! Makes 6 servings.

Note: Try Starrlight Mead Off-dry Pear Mead in this recipe next time for a completely different and delicious taste.

Charles Pace, employee
Starrlight Mead

Lemon, Wine, Vinegar Chicken

Chicken breast, bone-in (1½ pieces per person)

3 garlic cloves, divided

Olive oil

½ to ¾ pound fresh mushrooms, sliced

Wash and pat dry chicken breast, skin on. Cut in half. Sauté garlic in olive oil until brown. Add chicken, skin side down, and cook each side until brown. Remove chicken, discard grease. Return chicken to fry pan, brush top with olive oil, and add sliced mushrooms. Cover and cook 3 to 5 minutes.

Sauce:

2 garlic cloves

¼ cup fresh lemon juice

¼ cup red wine vinegar

½ cup Sauterne wine

2 cloves garlic, minced

½ teaspoon dried oregano

Combine all ingredients and add to pan. Simmer another 5 minutes. Serve over cooked white or brown rice.

Salvatore Ponticelli, owner's father
Carolina Balloon Adventures

Carolina Balloon Adventures

3028 Black Diamond Lane
East Bend
704-437-9673
www.usaballoon.com

Located just 16 miles west of Winston-Salem

Guests can experience first-hand the wonder of floating above the earth in a hot air balloon. Come fly with Captain Jack over the beautiful Yadkin Valley and get a bird's eye view of the rolling hills filled with wildlife, streams, lakes, ponds, trees and farms. Flights will take guests to heights from which one can see the hills of Tennessee and Virginia, Pilot Mountain, Hanging Rock, and the skyline of Winston-Salem. The balloons also fly low enough to gather leaves from the trees and talk to people on the ground. Come and experience North Carolina from a different prospective.

- Morning or afternoon flights weather permitting
- Dinner flights from a local winery
- Gift certificates
- Romantic weekend get away

Fettuccine with Chicken and Chapel Hill Creamery's Calvander Cheese

1 pound boneless chicken breasts,
   cut into 1-inch pieces
4 tablespoons olive oil, divided
1 cup chopped mushrooms
½ red bell pepper, diced
2 zucchini, chopped
½ teaspoon salt

1 teaspoon dried basil
2 cloves garlic, minced
½ cup chicken broth
8 ounces fettuccine
12 ounces Chapel Hill Creamery's
   Calvander cheese, grated

Sauté chicken in 2 tablespoons olive oil in large skillet 3 to 5 minutes until no longer pink. Remove and cover to keep warm. Add 1 tablespoon oil to pan and cook mushrooms and peppers 3 minutes. Add zucchini and cook 2 minutes, add salt, basil, garlic, broth, and cooked chicken. Reduce to simmer. Cook pasta al dente. Add ½ cup pasta water to skillet before draining. Quickly rinse in colander and shake off excess water. Pour pasta onto platter and toss with 1 tablespoon olive oil and 2 spoonfuls of Chapel Hill Creamery's Calvander cheese. Top with chicken mixture and add Calvander cheese for garnish.

Chapel Hill Creamery

Chapel Hill Creamery

615 Chapel Hill Creamery Road • Chapel Hill
iwww.chapelhillcreamery.com

This award-winning farmstead cheese producer makes a variety of distinctive cheeses using milk from its own herd of Jersey cows. Chapel Hill Creamery milks Jersey cows because they are well-suited for NC's warm climate and their rich milk produces high-quality, flavorful cheese. You will find Chapel Hill Creamery's cheeses at the Carrboro, Downtown Durham and Raleigh State farmers' markets and at many retail stores statewide. Chapel Hill Creamery is an Animal Welfare Approved farm and welcomes visitors during its spring and fall farm tours. Featured in Garden & Gun Magazine and Southern Living. Awarded "Best in Show" at the NC State Fair International Cheese Competition 2013, 2012 & 2011.

Follow on facebook.com/chapelhillcreamery and @CHCreameryNC

Stuffed Roasted Chicken Breast with Black Mission Fig Jam, Spinach and Goat Cheese

Black Mission Fig Jam:

2 or 3 tablespoons finely chopped
  onion
1½ teaspoons dry thyme
2 tablespoons sugar
Salt and black pepper to taste

⅓ cup red wine
1 cup diced dried Black Mission figs
1 tablespoon honey
1 tablespoon red wine vinegar

Sauté onion, thyme, sugar and salt and pepper until lightly browned. Add wine, figs, honey and vinegar and cook until mixture becomes a syrup. Let cool.

Chicken Breasts:

8 boneless, skinless chicken breasts
2 cups fresh spinach
1 clove garlic, minced
8 ounces goat cheese

Oil
¼ cup shallots
¼ cup white wine
1 tablespoon butter

Trim chicken breasts and flatten with a mallet. Lightly sauté spinach with garlic. Spread about 1 ounce each of jam and goat cheese and about 2 tablespoons wilted spinach on each breast. Start at 1 end and roll meat and filling and secure with a toothpick. Heat a little oil in sauté pan and lightly brown the chicken. Place on greased baking pan and bake about 20 minutes at 375° to finish cooking.

While chicken is in the oven make a simple pan sauce in the pan you used. Add some finely chopped shallots and cook until softened. Add a splash of white wine and cook until reduced by half. Add some butter and swirl until it melts. Slice chicken crosswise into medallions and place on serving plate. Drizzle with pan sauce.

Red Rocker Inn

Easy Chicken Casserole

3 to 4 cooked chicken breasts, chopped
1 (16-ounce) package wide egg noodles, cooked
1 (24-ounce) container sour cream
2 (10¾–ounce) cans cream of chicken soup
1 (8-ounce) package shredded Cheddar cheese
1 (8-ounce) package shredded mozzarella cheese
1 sleeve round buttery crackers, crushed
¼ cup butter, melted
2 tablespoons poppy seed

Combine chicken, noodles, sour cream, soup and cheeses in a large bowl. Pour into a lightly greased 3x13-inch baking dish. Mix together cracker crumbs and butter; sprinkle over top. Sprinkle poppy seed over cracker crumbs. Bake at 350° for 25 to 30 minutes or until crackers are crispy and golden and cheese is melted.

Swiss Bear Downtown Development

Historic Downtown New Bern:
A Main Street Success Story

Recognized for its "sense of place and walk-ability", visitors receive a warm welcome to historic New Bern and its beautifully revitalized downtown and waterfront. Due to an aggressive revitalization effort led by Swiss Bear Downtown Development Corporation, a private nonprofit, and in partnership with local government, the heart of this city is now a destination. Planned overall growth and many special events attract thousands of visitors throughout the year. Downtown offers shops, art galleries, coffee shops, restaurants, historic attractions and museums, a range of cultural activities, waterfront hotels and marinas, B&B accommodations, public parks, historic homes and churches and a waterfront convention center.

By emphasizing downtown's historic assets and waterfront development, downtown New Bern is an award-winning Main Street success story. For more information go to www.downtownnewbern.com.

Artichoke Chicken Bake

4 boneless, skinless chicken breast halves
Salt and pepper to taste
1 (14-ounce) can marinated artichokes, drained and chopped
¾ to 1 cup grated Parmesan cheese
¾ cup mayonnaise
1 dash garlic powder or 2 garlic cloves, optional

Preheat oven to 375°. Spray an 11x7-inch baking dish with nonstick cooking spray. Salt and pepper chicken breast halves and place in dish. In a bowl, combine artichoke hearts, Parmesan cheese, mayonnaise and garlic powder; mix well. Spread mixture over chicken breasts. Bake, uncovered, 30 to 35 minutes or until chicken juices run clear.

Nancy Hawley
MUMFEST, New Bern

Chicken and Stuffing Bake

1 package chicken-flavored Stovetop
   Stuffing
½ cup chopped celery
½ cup chopped onion
½ cup chopped carrot, optional
⅓ cup milk

1 (10¾-ounce) can cream of mushroom
   soup
1 teaspoon chopped parsley
6 skinless, boneless chicken breasts
Paprika

Prepare stuffing according to package, adding the vegetables with seasoning packet. Combine milk, soup and parsley; set aside. In a 2- or 3-quart shallow baking dish, arrange stuffing in center. Spoon thin layer of soup mixture on each side of stuffing. Arrange chicken over soup mixture, overlapping if needed. Sprinkle with paprika. Pour remaining soup mixture over chicken. Cover with foil and bake 15 minutes at 400°. Uncover and bake 10 minutes more or until chicken is fork tender. Stir sauce before serving. Yields 6 servings.

Judy Cavenaugh
North Carolina Poultry Jubilee

High Hampton Inn

Aussie Chicken Recipe

2 skinless, boneless chicken breast halves, pounded to ½-inch thickness
1 teaspoon seasoning salt
3 slices bacon, cut in half
¼ cup prepared mustard
¼ cup honey
2 tablespoons light corn syrup
2 tablespoons mayonnaise
1½ teaspoons dried onion flakes
½ cup sliced mushrooms
1 cup shredded Colby-Monterey Jack cheese
1 tablespoon chopped fresh parsley

Rub chicken breasts with seasoning salt and refrigerate 30 minutes. Preheat oven to 350°. Place bacon in a large, deep skillet. Cook over medium-high heat until crisp. Set aside. Do not clean skillet. In medium bowl, combine mustard, honey, corn syrup, mayonnaise and dried onion flakes. Remove half of sauce, cover and refrigerate to serve later. Reheat skillet over medium heat. Place breasts in skillet and sauté 3 to 5 minutes per side or until browned. Remove from skillet and place in a 9x13-inch baking dish. Apply the honey mustard sauce to each breast, and then layer with mushrooms and bacon. Sprinkle with cheese. Bake 15 minutes or until cheese is melted and chicken juices run clear. Garnish with parsley and serve with reserved honey mustard sauce.

Danielle Glynn
MUMFEST, New Bern

Crispy Chicken

1½ cups crushed Rice Krispies
2 tablespoons flour
1 teaspoon dried basil, oregano or Italian seasoning (use whatever you have on hand)

½ teaspoon salt
½ teaspoon garlic powder
¼ cup melted butter
4 boneless, skinless chicken breast halves or 8 chicken tenderloins

In a zip-close bag, combine Rice Krispies, flour, seasoning of your choice, salt, and garlic powder. With a rolling pin or your hands, crush Rice Krispies. Melt butter in a small dish. Dip chicken in butter, coating both sides. Add chicken to zip-close bag and shake to evenly coat. Arrange chicken pieces in a 9x13-inch baking dish. Drizzle with remaining butter. Bake at 400° for 20 to 25 minutes. I like to move the baking dish to the top rack for another 10 minutes so the chicken gets nice and brown and crispy.

Mandy James
North Carolina Poultry Jubilee

Apple Hill Farm

Mandy's Famous Spicy Chicken Enchiladas

1 small onion, chopped
1 clove garlic, minced
1 tablespoon oil
1 pound boneless, skinless chicken
   breasts, cooked and shredded
1½ cups salsa, divided
1 (4-ounce) package cream cheese
1 tablespoon cilantro, chopped

1 teaspoon ground cumin
½ cup shredded Cheddar cheese,
   divided
½ cup Monterey Jack cheese,
   shredded, divided
1 (4-ounce) can green chiles or
   jalapeños, drained and chopped
8 flour tortillas

Cook and stir onion and garlic in hot oil in large skillet on medium heat 2 minutes. Add chicken, ¼ cup salsa, cream cheese, cilantro and cumin. Cook until heated through, stirring occasionally. Add ¼ cup Cheddar cheese, ¼ cup Monterey Jack cheese and green chiles; mix well. Remove from heat. In pan, divide mixture into 8 equal parts. Lightly heat tortillas, a couple at a time, on stove or in microwave for 10 seconds. (They don't tear and are easier to fold when heated.) Spoon mixture onto each tortilla as they are heated; roll up. Place seam-side down in a 13x9-inch baking dish. Top with remaining salsa and cheeses. Bake at 350° for 15 to 20 minutes or until heated through and top is bubbly. I usually double this recipe and stretch my mixture for 20 enchiladas instead of 16. Great with sour cream!

Mandy James
North Carolina Poultry Jubilee

Chicken Parmesan

4 boneless Buffalo Creek Farm pastured chicken breasts
¼ cup grated Buffalo Creek Farm Rock House Parmesan-style Goat Cheese
1 cup goat milk yogurt
1 teaspoon garlic powder
1 to 1½ teaspoons seasoning salt
½ teaspoon pepper

Place chicken breasts in single layer in baking dish. Mix remaining ingredients and spread evenly over chicken. Bake at 375° for 45 minutes.

Buffalo Creek Farm and Creamery

Company's Coming Chicken

1 (8-ounce) package cream cheese, softened
3 cups cooked boneless chicken breast, shredded
¼ cup chicken broth
½ teaspoon salt
½ teaspoon black pepper
½ cup sour cream
1 cup pecans
2 cups herb seasoned stuffing mix
1 (8-ounce) can crescent rolls
½ stick butter, melted

With clean hands, mix together cream cheese, chicken, broth, salt, pepper and sour cream until well blended and chicken is very fine. Mix together pecans and stuffing mix and process in blender until fine. Open crescent rolls and unroll. Flatten and cut into 36 equal rectangles and stretch to 3-inch squares. Place 1 tablespoon chicken mixture in center of dough. Pull all sides together to form a ball and seal any open edges. Dip into butter and roll in pecan stuffing mixture. Repeat until all squares have been used. Place side by side in a 9x13-inch glass baking dish that has been coated with butter. Bake uncovered at 350° for 45 minutes. Wonderful served with cranberry salad, mixed greens and wild rice. Pair this hearty dish with Laurel Gray Vineyards Barrel Fermented Chardonnay.

Laurel Gray Vineyards

Crockpot Chicken Divan

1 (20-ounce) package frozen
    broccoli spears
6 chicken breasts
2 cups mayonnaise

2 (10¾-ounce) cans cream of
    chicken soup
2 teaspoons lemon juice

Place broccoli in crockpot. Top off broccoli with chicken. Mix together mayonnaise, soup and lemon juice. Pour over chicken. Cover and cook on low 8 hours.

Amy Johnson
North Carolina Poultry Jubilee

North Carolina Poultry Jubilee

1st weekend in October

Main Street • Rosehill
www.NCPoultryJubilee.com

The North Carolina Poultry Jubilee is held every year in Rose Hill, home of "The World's Largest Frying Pan." On Jubilee weekend, before sunrise on Saturday morning, volunteers from the Rose Hill Fire Department and surrounding areas begin prepping the frying pan for frying approximately 1500 to 2,000 pieces of chicken. The frying pan is a star attraction, but there is so much more to see and do at NC Poultry Jubilee. On Friday night beginning at 6pm to 11pm there are Carnival rides, a Chicken Wing Cook-Off, live music, a street dance, a beer and wine garden, and more. On Saturday beginning at 11am to 11pm there is a parade, carnival rides, fried chicken plates, arts and crafts vendors, food vendors, beer and wine garden, local entertainment, live beach music bands, a street dance, wing eating contest and much more.

Pecan Crusted Chicken

6 (6-ounce) chicken breasts
2 cups coarse chopped pecans
2 cups fine breadcrumbs
2 cups white wine

4 tablespoons Dijon mustard, divided
¼ cup whipping cream
¼ cup chicken broth

Wash and dry chicken; set aside. Combine pecans and breadcrumbs, mixing well. Combine white wine and 3 tablespoons Dijon mustard together. Roll chicken breast in wine mixture, then into the fine breadcrumbs. Bake chicken at 350° for 45 to 60 minutes or until juices run clear. Time will depend on oven and number of chicken breasts.

Champagne Cream Sauce:

In a sauce pan over medium-high heat, add whipping cream, chicken stock and remaining Dijon mustard. Bring almost to a boil, stirring constantly. Pour over cooked chicken breasts and return to oven to heat and to brown the cream sauce slightly. Serve hot.

Red, White and Bluegrass Festival

June

Catawba Meadows Park • Morganton
www.redwhiteandbluegrassfestival.com

ISTOCK/DON BAYLEY

The Red, White and Bluegrass Festival hosts the hottest names in bluegrass. This four-day long event has camping on site, a camp for kids, instrument sales, terrific food and an amazing firework display. This event is fun for music buffs and people who just love camping. Bring the whole family for an old-fashioned, American-style celebration.

Poppy Seed Chicken

4 skinless, boneless chicken breast halves, cooked and cubed or shredded
1 (10½-ounce) can condensed cream of chicken soup
1 (10½ ounce) can cream of mushroom soup
1 (8-ounce) container sour cream
1 (8-ounce) package buttery round crackers, crushed (about 40 crackers)
1 tablespoon poppy seeds
½ cup melted butter

Preheat oven to 350°. Mix chicken with undiluted soups and sour cream. Stir until well blended. Transfer mixture to 9x13-inch baking dish. In a separate bowl, combine crushed crackers with poppy seeds. Stir melted butter into cracker mixture and spread evenly over chicken. Bake 30 minutes or until heated through and lightly browned on top.

Debby Scott
North Carolina Poultry Jubilee

Chicken Supreme

2 cups herb-flavored stuffing
½ cup melted butter
¼ cup finely chopped onion
1 (10¾-ounce) can cream of chicken soup

¼ cup water or chicken stock
4 to 6 boneless, skinless chicken breasts
4 to 6 slices Swiss cheese

Mix stuffing, melted butter and onion together and set aside. Dilute soup with water or stock.

On baking sheet with rimmed edge, place chicken in a row. Cover with cheese and then pour soup over all. Sprinkle stuffing mixture over soup. Place in 325° oven and bake 1½ hours.

Sonya Snyder, Town of Cary Parks,
Recreation and Cultural Resource Department
Cary Kite Festival

Homemade Chicken Pastry

1 chicken
5 cups self-rising flour plus more for rolling
1 egg
⅔ cup hot (not boiling) water

Cook chicken in water to cover until done, salt and pepper to taste. Remove chicken from pot. Keep broth at a simmer. Sift flour into a large bowl and make a hole in the center of flour. Break egg into the hole and add half the hot water. Mix thoroughly with surrounding flour. Add remaining water, mix and knead the flour until it looks like bread dough. Sprinkle counter with flour and roll pastry thin. Cut pastry into pieces. Sprinkle flour on a platter and put the pastry on it in order to dry for a while. When dry, drop 1 piece at a time into boiling broth. Pull chicken off bones, put some back in pot with pastry.

Carrie Jean Autry of Autryville
Hollerin' Heritage Festival

The Inn at Elk River

Better than KFC Pot Pie

2 potatoes, peeled and chopped
⅔ cup frozen green peas
⅔ cup frozen carrot slices
2 tablespoons finely chopped onion
2 (10¾-ounce) cans cream of chicken soup
1 (12-ounce) can evaporated milk
2 cups cooked, chopped chicken
Dash salt and pepper
Dash MSG, optional
Pillsbury ready-to-use refrigerated piecrusts

Place potatoes, peas, carrots and onion in a bowl with a small amount of water and cook in microwave until tender. Drain vegetables. In a bowl combine cooked vegetables and chicken. Add soup, milk and seasonings. Put in a greased 9x13-inch pan and top with piecrusts. Cut a few vent holes in crust. Bake at 375° for 25 to 30 minutes or until crust is brown and pie is bubbly.

Sonya Snyder, Town of Cary Parks,
Recreation and Cultural Resource Department
Cary Kite Festival

Chicken Pot Pie

1 whole chicken, cooked and
   de-boned
1 (14.5-ounce) peas and carrots,
   drained (may use frozen)

1½ cup cooked and cubed potatoes
1 (10¾-ounce) can cream of celery soup
1 (14-ounce) can chicken broth
2 boiled eggs, chopped

Spray large casserole dish with non-stick cooking spray and place cut chicken in dish. Add peas and carrots and potatoes. In separate bowl, combine celery soup, chicken broth, and chopped eggs; mix well. Pour over chicken/vegetable mixture.

Topping:

1 cup flour
½ cup melted butter

1 cup milk

Combine flour and butter; mix well. Gradually add milk to avoid lumping. Pour over the top of chicken mixture. DO NOT STIR. Bake at 375° for 30 to 35 minutes or until crust is golden brown.

Jackie Hanson
Mills Spring Farm Store

Wild Turkey

1 turkey
1 stick butter
1½ pounds fatback

3 stalks celery
Salt and pepper

Place turkey in a large pot and cover with water. Add butter, fatback and celery. Bring to a boil. Add salt and pepper to taste. Cook 20 minutes per pound on medium-high on top of stove.

Creedmoor Music Festival

Cranberry Relish

1 (14-ounce) can whole-berry cranberry sauce
2 stalks celery, finely chopped
½ cup pecans, finely chopped
1 orange, peeled and finely chopped
½ cup dried cranberries

Combine all ingredients and refrigerator at least 2 hours before serving. This is good with turkey and roast pork.

Evelyn McNeill Waddell
Columbus County Community Farmers Market

Applesauce Meat Loaf

Meatloaf:

1 egg, beaten
½ cup applesauce
2 tablespoons chopped onion
½ teaspoon salt
¼ teaspoon black pepper

1 teaspoon dried celery flakes
1 pound lean ground beef
1½ cups soft breadcrumbs
1 teaspoon mustard

Combine above ingredients and blend thoroughly. Place in greased loaf pan.

Sauce:

½ cup applesauce
1 tablespoon brown sugar

2 teaspoons cider vinegar
½ teaspoon mustard

Mix all sauce ingredients. Make a depression down middle of meatloaf with a spoon and pour in sauce. Bake at 350° for 1 hour.

Brushy Mountain Ruritan Club
Brushy Mountain Apple Festival

Southern Sisters

Though Southern Sisters just opened in 2012, the restaurant, chef and owners quickly became media darlings in the region because of their great food, great atmosphere and great menu. Southern Sisters' co-owner Joy Thompson is a regular on local television news shows giving cooking tips while she and the restaurant have also been featured multiple times on national food programs.

Meatloaf

2 pounds ground beef
2 teaspoon salt
½ teaspoon black pepper
1 cup chopped onion
1 cup chopped green bell pepper
2 eggs, lightly beaten

1 (16-ounce) can diced tomatoes,
 drained
1 cup crushed panko breadcrumbs
½ cup Heinz 57 sauce
½ cup ketchup

Mix all ingredients well, pat into loaf pan and bake at 375° for 45 to 55 minutes.

Topping:

⅔ cup ketchup
4 tablespoons brown sugar

2 tablespoons mustard

Mix together topping ingredients and spread over top of loaf when there is 15 minutes left to cook.

Southern Sisters Restaurant & Grille
336-474-8620 • www.southernsisters.info
Thomasville Tourism

Thomasville Tourism

800-611-9907
www.thomasvilletourism.com

The hard work that goes into producing the finest quality furniture in the world is the same type of work Thomasville puts into its festivals. Be sure to visit the Chair City conveniently located in the center of North Carolina along Interstate 85.

Some of the annual Chair City Festivals:

May • 1st Saturday
Spring Daze Festival with plants, outdoor yard accessories, games, and music

May • Memorial Day Weekend
The Southeastern United States' largest Memorial Day Parade and Celebration

July 4th
Baseball and fireworks with the Hi Toms baseball team

September • Last Saturday
Everybody's Day is the oldest continuous festival in North Carolina and it has something for everybody!

October • 1st Friday and Saturday
Chair City Antiques Festival

November • Saturday before Thanksgiving
Thomasville Christmas Parade

Blackberry Mead Crockpot Pot Roast

½ bottle Starrlight Mead Blackberry Off-dry Mead
2 cloves garlic, minced
2 sprigs fresh rosemary, divided
2 pounds chuck roast
1 medium onion, diced
1 tablespoon oil
Salt and pepper to taste
3 to 5 large carrots, cut into large chunks
6 to 10 new potatoes

Add mead, garlic and 1 sprig rosemary to a zip-close bag. Add roast and marinate 12 to 24 hours in refrigerator. Remove meat from marinade and pat dry. Pour marinade into crockpot. Sauté onion in oil until translucent. Add to crockpot. Salt and pepper the roast. Brown each side of roast in hot skillet and add to crockpot along with the carrots and potatoes. Add remaining sprig of rosemary. Cover and cook on low 10 to 12 hours or high 5 to 6 hours.

Ben Starr, owner
Starrlight Mead

Marinated Beef Tips

1 cup cooking sherry
¾ cup Wesson oil
¾ cup soy sauce
2 pounds beef tips

1 small onion, chopped
1 (6.5-ounce) can sliced mushrooms,
 drained
Dash black pepper

Mix together sherry, oil and soy sauce. Stir in beef tips, onion, mushrooms and pepper. Cover and refrigerate at least 8 hours. Bake in 450° oven, uncovered, 45 minutes.

Linda Gough
Shelton Vineyards

Bourbon-Glazed Rib-Eyes

1 tablespoon kosher salt
1 tablespoon fresh cracked pepper
1 tablespoon garlic powder

1 tablespoon dried onion
1 teaspoon blackening seasoning
4 (14-ounce) thick-cut rib-eye steaks

Mix seasonings together and dredge steaks. Wrap tightly in plastic wrap and refrigerate 12 hours.

Bourbon Glaze:

1 tablespoon crushed garlic
1 stick melted butter
Pinch salt and pepper

½ cup brown sugar
½ cup local honey
3 ounces Maker's Mark bourbon

Sauté garlic in butter over medium heat until almost brown. Add sugar. Once sugar is melted add honey. Stir, remove from heat and when cool, whisk in bourbon.

Unwrap steaks; do not brush off the rub. Grill steaks to desired doneness. When steaks are flipped, generously apply glaze. Makes 4 servings.

Courtesy of Olde Hickory Station • 828-322-2356
Hickory Oktoberfest

Hoisin-Glazed Short Ribs

3 to 4 pounds short ribs, boneless or bone-in
Salt and pepper
1 gallon beef stock or broth
Hoisin sauce (available at well-stocked grocery stores or Asian markets)

Season meat with salt and pepper and let sit 30 minutes. Grill meat with a nice char to seal in juices.

Place in deep pan, cover with stock. Bring to simmer on top of stove, and then place in 300° oven and cook, covered, 1½ to 2 hours until tender. If desired can be cooked in crockpot overnight on low setting.

Let cool in liquid to absorb flavor. Remove and slice into portion sizes. Place in large saucepan and add 2 tablespoons hoisin sauce and 1 cup stock left over from cooking. Slowly bring to a simmer and reduce liquid to glaze consistency. May add soft butter to finish sauce if desired. Makes 4 servings.

Recipe courtesy of Josh's On Union Square • 828-324-5674
Hickory Oktoberfest

Hickory Oktoberfest

2nd weekend in October

828-322-1121
www.hickoryoktoberfest.com

Every fall Hickory celebrates its German heritage with Oktoberfest. Ranked #10 on Facebook among the nation's 500 Oktoberfest events, Hickory offers a weekend to remember. For nearly 30 years, artisans and craftsmen have gathered on Union Square for the FREE three-day festival which attracts more than 95,000 guests to Downtown Hickory. More than 100 vendors line the streets, and the food court features a variety of cuisine with everything from traditional German fare to funnel cakes and cotton candy. Grab a bratwurst and a Bavarian apple pie and visit the traditional German beer garden for polka in the Pavilion. Kidsfest offers carnival games, face painting, and amusement rides for the entire family. Four stages feature live entertainment with a variety of sounds from rock to Americana to blues to jazz. Visit the website to learn more about Hickory's Oktoberfest.

24-Hour Braised Bone-in Short Ribs

6 bone-in short ribs
Kosher salt and pepper to taste
Extra-virgin olive oil
1 large Spanish onion, cut into
  ½-inch pieces
2 ribs celery, cut into ½-inch pieces
2 carrots, peeled and cut into ½-inch
  pieces

2 cloves garlic, smashed
½ cup tomato paste
2 cups red wine
2 cups veal stock
1 bunch fresh thyme
2 bay leaves

Season each short rib generously with salt and pepper. Coat an oven-safe pot large enough to accommodate all the meat and vegetables with olive oil and bring to a high heat. Add short ribs and brown very well, about 2 to 3 minutes per side. Do not overcrowd pan; cook in batches if necessary. Preheat oven to 375°. When short ribs are very brown on all sides, remove from pan. Drain the fat. Coat bottom of same pan with fresh oil and add the vegetables. Season vegetables generously with salt and brown until they are caramelized, approximately 5 to 7 minutes. Add tomato paste. Brown tomato paste 4 to 5 minutes. Add wine and scrape browned bits from bottom of pan. Lower heat if vegetables start to caramelize too much. Reduce liquid by half. Return short ribs to the pan and add enough veal stock to just about cover the meat. Add thyme bundle and bay leaves. Cover pan and place in preheated oven 3 hours. Check periodically during the cooking process and add more water if needed. Remove lid during the last 20 minutes of cooking to let things get nice and brown and to reduce the sauce. When done the meat should be very tender but not falling apart. Serve with the braising liquid.

Tour De Food
Recipe Courtesy of Mimosa Grill,
a stop on Tour De Food in Charlotte
704-375-9715 • www.harpersgroup.com
336-406-6294 www.tourdefood.net

Tour De Food

Eat · Drink · Walk

Apple Butter Barbecue Spareribs

4 pounds pork spareribs
Salt and black pepper
1 onion, quartered
16 ounces apple butter
1 (18-ounce) bottle barbecue sauce

Preheat oven to 350°. Sprinkle ribs generously with salt and pepper. Place on a rimmed baking sheet. Bake 30 minutes; drain. Slice ribs into serving-size pieces and place in a crockpot. Add remaining ingredients. Cover and cook on low 8 hours. Or place in a large heavy pot, cover and cook over low heat on stovetop for how long. Makes 4 to 6 servings.

Bonnie Schmink
The Orchard at Altapass

Barbeque Sauce

1 gallon apple cider vinegar
1 (16-ounce) box brown sugar
1 (14-ounce) bottle of ketchup
Salt, pepper and red pepper flakes to taste

Mix all ingredients together in saucepan and bring to boil. Simmer for approximately 10 minutes. Store in refrigerator. Great for grilling!

Noah Jackson of Spivey's Corner
Hollerin' Heritage Festival

Barbecue Pork Chops

4 bone-in pork loin chops
2 teaspoons vegetable oil
1 medium green pepper, chopped
⅔ cup chopped celery
⅓ cup chopped onion

1 cup ketchup
¼ cup packed brown sugar
¼ cup reduced-sodium chicken broth
2 tablespoons chili powder

In a large nonstick skillet, brown pork chops in oil over medium-high heat. Remove chops and set aside. Add green pepper, celery and onion to skillet; cook and stir until vegetables begin to soften. Return pork chops to pan. In a bowl, combine ketchup, brown sugar, broth and chili powder. Pour over chops and vegetables. Bring to a boil. Reduce heat; cover and simmer 30 minutes or until meat is tender.

Sterling Silver Boneless Pork Loin Crusted with Bakers' Southern Cajun Peanuts

1 (3-pound) fresh, boneless, Sterling Silver pork loin, rinsed and patted dry
Black pepper
1 teaspoon olive oil
3 eggs beaten to a fluffy whip
3 cups Bakers' Southern Cajun Peanuts, rough chop

Season pork loin with black pepper. Heat a sauté pan over medium heat. Add oil to center of pan and when oil is hot, quickly brown pork loin on each side. Remove and let rest.

Preheat oven to 350°. Place pork loin on baking sheet and lightly brush top with egg wash. Sprinkle with chopped peanuts, gently pressing them into meat. Bake 15 minutes or until meat thermometer reaches internal temperature of 145° when inserted into center of loin. Remove from oven and let rest 8 minutes. Slice and serve with your favorite Southern vegetable. Makes 6 servings.

*Bakers' Southern Traditions with
Chef Michael Giletto as seen on Food Network*

Roasted Pork Tenderloin

3 pork tenderloins (about 1½ pounds each)
2 teaspoons kosher salt
½ teaspoon freshly ground black pepper
3 tablespoons olive oil
Bourbon Glaze (recipe follows)
Braised Red Cabbage (see page 106)

Preheat oven to 400°. Season pork with salt and pepper. Heat olive oil in ovenproof skillet over high heat and sear pork on all sides. Place skillet in oven and roast pork 8 to 10 minutes. Let meat rest 5 minutes. Slicing on the diagonal, cut each tenderloin into 4 or 5 pieces.

Bourbon Glaze:

1 tablespoon olive oil
2 shallots, chopped
2 cloves garlic, chopped
2 cups brown sugar
¾ cup balsamic vinegar
½ cup red wine
½ cup apple cider
2 teaspoons green peppercorns (found at specialty food stores)
1 bay leaf
1 cup seeded and chopped plum tomatoes
½ cup chopped red bell pepper
5 sprigs Italian parsley
3 tablespoons soy sauce
1½ ounces bourbon

In a medium pot, heat oil over medium heat and add shallots and garlic. Cook until soft but not browned. Add sugar, vinegar, wine, cider, green peppercorns, bay leaf, tomatoes, red pepper, parsley and soy sauce. Simmer until reduced by half. Strain sauce and add bourbon. Serve warm over sliced pork tenderloin or chops. Makes 2 cups sauce.

Creedmoor Music Festival

Caribbean Pork Chops with Sherried Black Beans

Sherried Black Beans:

1 red onion, chopped

1 red pepper, chopped

1 yellow pepper, chopped

1 carrot, peeled and chopped

1 tablespoon chopped garlic

1 tablespoon chopped fresh ginger

4 slices bacon, crisped and chopped

1 jalapeño, seeded and chopped

1 tablespoon cumin powder

1 tablespoon chili powder

1 tablespoon paprika

1 tablespoon allspice

1 teaspoon cayenne pepper

¼ cup sherry vinegar

¾ cup sherry

2 (14-ounce) cans black beans, drained

Chicken stock

Sauté onion, peppers and carrot until golden, add garlic and ginger and sauté 1 minute longer. not sure when to add bacon and jalapeño Add bacon, jalapeño and spices and toss for 1 minute then add vinegar and sherry and reduce by half. Stir in beans, then add chicken stock to just cover. Bring to a boil; reduce heat and simmer for 30 minutes until sauce thickens.

Carribbean Pork Chops:

4 bone-in thick-cut pork chops

Dry Jamaican jerk seasoning

Juice of 1 lime

1 teaspoon tamarind paste

1 tablespoon brown sugar

1 ripe banana, chopped

Dust pork chops with jerk seasoning and grill to medium; remove to rest for 5 minutes. Combine lime juice, tamarind and brown sugar, toss with banana. Place beans on plate, top with a chop and dress with banana mixture. Serve with Adagio Vineyards Chaconne.

Adagio Vineyards

Chorizo Stuffed Pork Chop

1 (12-ounce) pork chop
Salt and pepper
½ lime

¼ cup Brie-style cheese, sliced
¼ cup chorizo, cooked and crumbled
¼ cup arugula, chopped

Preheat oven to 350°. Heat skillet to medium high. Rub pork chop with salt and pepper. Squeeze juice from the half lime on both sides of chop. Pan sear chop, approximately 30 seconds per side. Remove from skillet and let cool a few minutes. Make a 2-inch incision on 1 side of pork chop along the fat cap. Do not cut all the way through; you are making a pocket for the filling. Place sliced Brie inside chop, add chorizo and arugula. Push chorizo and arugula back into the chop so they do not fall out when cooking. Bake chop, covered, 20 to 25 minutes.

Hickory Nut Gap Farm

Hickory Nut Gap Farm

57 Sugar Hollow Road
Fairview
828-628-1027
www.hickorynutgapfarm.com

Hickory Nut Gap Farm is a family owned and operated farm that has spanned generations. They produce 100% grassfed beef, pasture raised pork, and pasture raised chicken, along with cured meats, certified organic apples, mushrooms, and berries. Additionally, they offer a variety of local products in the farm store. But that is not all! There are guided tours of the animals, berries, orchard, and bees, the farm is available for school field trips, and there is a seasonal open house four times a year. Guests can pick their own berries, picnic by the creek, and visit some of the animals. The fall offers hay rides, horse rides, a corn maze, and a 40-foot culvert slide. Hickory Nut Gap Farm is a haven for people who seek whole food, wholesomeness, and a simpler way of life. Call or visit their website for hours, tour information, and current activity dates.

Shredded Pork Tacos with Mora Salsa Fresca

1 (4- to 5-pound) Boston butt roast
2 teaspoons chili powder
2 teaspoons cumin
2 teaspoons cayenne powder
1 teaspoon paprika
Salt and pepper to taste

1 (10-ounce) can tomatoes with green chilies
1 or 2 dried pasilla chiles, stems removed
1 or 2 shots of tequila (either in the dish or for the cook, optional)

Place pork roast in crockpot. Add seasoning, tomatoes and pasilla chiles. Add water to cover by two thirds. Add tequila if using. Cook on high 3 to 4 hours; turn to low and cook until tender, typically 6 hours depending on cooker and size of roast. Optionally, you can cook on high overnight or during the day but leaving a crockpot unattended can be dangerous!

When pork is tender to the point of falling apart, turn off crockpot and remove any remaining large chunks of bone and/or fat. Serve shredded pork on corn taco shells or soft tortillas topped with shredded lettuce, Mora Salsa Fresca, shredded cheese, chopped cilantro and/or fresh guacamole. Pairs well with a Rioja, Shiraz or other red wine with body and a bit of spice.

Mora Salsa Fresca:

6 Roma tomatoes, diced
¾ red onion, finely chopped
⅔ quart blackberries, chopped
2 tablespoons vinegar
Juice of 6 small or 4 large limes

1 teaspoon cumin
½ cup cilantro, rinsed and chopped
1 or 2 finely chopped jalapeño peppers, seeds removed (optional)
Salt to taste

Combine ingredients in sealable container; let marinate for 2-plus hours.

North Carolina Blackberry Festival

Pasole

1 to 2 pounds pork roast	2 to 3 tablespoons flour
¼ cup cooking oil	3 (15-ounce) cans white hominy
1 medium onion, chopped	3 (15-ounce) cans yellow hominy
½ cup diced green chiles, canned or frozen	2 chopped garlic cloves
	2 tablespoons red pepper sauce

Cook pork in oil in skillet until almost done. Add onion and chiles and cook until onions are clear. Add oil if needed. Add flour and stir. Add juice from hominy and water, if needed, to make thick gravy. Heat drained hominy in large saucepan along with garlic and pepper sauce. Add pork mixture to hominy and bring to a slow boil. Simmer 15 to 20 minutes. Makes 4 to 6 servings.

Qualla Arts and Crafts Mutual

LEAF

Apple-Sausage-Cabbage Baked Casserole

1 pound pork sausage
3 medium apples, cored and sliced
1 medium cabbage, shredded

Salt, optional
1 tablespoon vinegar

Shape sausage into flat cakes. Fry in a skillet until crisp. In a greased baking dish, arrange layers of apples and cabbage, salting each layer lightly if desired. Place sausage cakes on top. Pour vinegar into hot sausage grease left in skillet; stir. Pour over top layers. Cover and bake at 350° about 45 minutes.

Brushy Mountain Ruritan Club
Brushy Mountain Apple Festival

Brushy Mountain Apple Festival

1st Saturday in October • 8am to 5pm

Downtown North Wilkesboro
336-921-3499
www.applefestival.net

The annual Brushy Mountain Apple Festival began in 1978 by the Brushy Mountain Ruritan Club as a fundraising project. It is a major fundraising event for over 100 civic, churches, and other non-profit organizations. One of the largest arts & crafts festivals in the Eastern US, it ranks among the Southeast Tourism Society's "Top 20 Events." During this free-admission family event boasting four music stages, the streets come alive with over 450 crafters, food vendors, Appalachian heritage exhibitors, and apple growers offering fresh apples, cider, and a host of apple products for sale. As one walks through the festival, the sounds of the Appalachian dulcimers, the smell of many freshly prepared foods, and the chatter of artisans demonstrating woodcarving, chair making, pottery throwing, soap making, and quilting entice young and old to enjoy the rich heritage of the mountains. So come join the Brushy Mountain Ruritan Club in celebrating fall in the foothills!

Pierogie Casserole

10 cups sauerkraut
2 pounds Polish sausage, cut into
    bite-size pieces
4 large yellow onions sliced thin
30 pierogies
½ cup caraway seeds
1 cup butter, melted

Rinse sauerkraut under water and drain. Place half of sauerkraut on bottom of a deep-dish casserole. Layer sausage, onions, pierogies and caraway seeds on top. Pour melted butter over everything and cover with other half of sauerkraut. Bake at 325° for 1 hour. Serves 10.

Erik D. Valenta
Catawba Science Center

Braised Lamb Shanks

4 lamb shanks, about 1 pound each
Flour seasoned with salt and pepper
Olive oil
1 (14-ounce) can diced tomatoes in
    juice
1 small onion, diced
1 cup chopped celery
2 carrots, peeled and chopped
1 cup dry white wine
1 teaspoon each oregano and chopped
    garlic
1 bay leaf
Chopped parsley for garnish

Dredge lamb shanks in seasoned flour. Heat olive oil in heavy skillet or Dutch oven. Brown shanks on all sides. Combine tomatoes and remaining ingredients and pour over shanks. Cover pan and braise at 300° for 3 hours or more, until meat is very tender, almost falling off the bone.

Remove the shanks to a platter and spoon the vegetable gravy over top. Sprinkle with chopped parsley.

Fryemont Inn

Shepherd's Soufflé

4 tablespoons butter, divided
1 cup fresh breadcrumbs
1½ cups heavy cream
5 ounces Buffalo Creek's Farm Plain Chevre, divided
2 cups cold, cooked, finely chopped Buffalo Creek Farm pastured
  leg of lamb
½ cup golden raisins
1 teaspoon yellow mustard
½ teaspoon paprika
1 teaspoon black pepper
3 Buffalo Creek Farm pastured eggs, separated
2 tablespoons butter
2 tablespoons chopped fresh parsley

Preheat oven to 350°. Rub inside of an 8-inch soufflé mold with 2 tablespoons butter. Coat mold with breadcrumbs, tap out excess and reserve.

In a large, heavy-bottomed saucepan, heat cream, reserved breadcrumbs, 2 ounces chevre and remaining butter. Cook until thickened. Remove from heat and add chopped lamb, raisins, mustard, seasonings and beaten egg yolks.

In a separate bowl, beat egg whites until stiff, then carefully fold whites and remaining chevre into meat mixture. Turn into prepared baking dish. Place in a 9x13-inch metal baking pan. Add enough hot water to outer pan to come halfway up sides of soufflé dish. Bake 35 minutes or until soufflé is puffed and golden brown on top and soft set in center.

Nikki Miller
Buffalo Creek Farm and Creamery

Slow-Cooker Venison Roast

3 pound venison roast
1 (10.5-ounce) can cream of mushroom soup
1 (10.5-ounce) can hot water
1 envelope Lipton Onion Soup Mix
1 teaspoon steak seasoning

Place roast in crock pot. Combine cream of mushroom and water; mix well. Pour over venison roast. Sprinkle with Lipton Onion Soup mix and steak seasoning. Cook on high 8 hours. May keep on low setting until ready to serve.

Wild Meat Festival

August

4 Court Street
Robbinsonville
828-479-3250
www.townofrobbinsville.com

ISTOCK/MATT GIBSON

There are some great wild game cooks in Graham County! The Wild Meat Festival There is a venison cook-off, a youth target shooting competition, and a 5k run and fun run. The popular "Taste of the Wild" gives visitors an opportunity to taste wild boar, deer, bear and quail. The Wild Meat Festival highlights the skills, talents, and traditions of mountain people and to share these with children and visitors.

Bison Pot Roast

¼ cup flour
1 tablespoon plus 2 teaspoons salt
1¼ teaspoons pepper
2 tablespoons shortening
1 (4-pound) bison chuck roast
1 (5-ounce) jar horseradish

2 cups water
8 small onions
8 small potatoes, pared and halved
8 medium carrots, halved crosswise
   and lengthwise

Sift together flour, salt and pepper. Rub mixture on meat, coating thoroughly. Melt shortening in large skillet or Dutch oven over medium heat. Brown meat on all sides, about 15 minutes. Reduce heat; spread horseradish on both sides of meat. Add water; cover tightly and simmer on top of range or in 275° oven 2 to 3 hours. Add vegetables and cook another hour or until meat and vegetables are tender.

Carolina Bison Farm

Carolina Bison Farm

828-236-1659
www.carolinabison.com

Located in the Blue Ridge Mountains of Western North Carolina, Carolina Bison raises its herd on top-quality grasses and pure mountain spring water. Bison graze freely on hundreds of open pasture acreage, reminiscent of the original native herds. Founded by author, lecturer, and whole-health practitioner Dr. Frank J. King, Jr. in 1985, Carolina Bison is one of the largest bison ranches in the Southeastern region. With a mission to improve the health of his patients naturally, Dr. King began prescribing bison meat with astonishing results. Noticing such dramatic improvements on a diet of bison, Dr. King continued to extend the size of his personal herd. Driven by the great history of the American Bison, he became committed to educating the public on the endless benefits of bison. Securing the future for these impressive animals remains an important agenda for Dr. King and his family. Call or visit the website for tour schedules, store ours and more.

Bison Lasagna

1 (14-ounce) can whole tomatoes
1 (8-ounce) can tomato sauce
1 (6-ounce) can tomato paste
Pepper to taste
1½ teaspoons oregano
1 teaspoon onion salt
Olive oil
1 cup chopped onion
1 clove garlic, minced

2 pounds lean ground bison
Salt to taste
1 package lasagna noodles
2 (8-ounce) packages sliced
  mozzarella cheese
2 (8-ounce) packages sliced
  Muenster cheese
¾ pound small-curd cottage cheese
¾ cup grated Parmesan cheese

In a large crockpot, simmer tomatoes, tomato sauce, tomato paste, pepper, oregano and onion salt. Leave lid of crockpot ajar to avoid excess moisture. In separate pan heat olive oil and add onion, garlic, ground bison and salt. Brown meat; drain excess oil. Add mixture to sauce. Simmer several hours, uncovered. Cook lasagna noodles according to directions, drain. Layer noodles, both types of sliced cheese, cottage cheese and sauce. Bake at 350° for 45 minutes. Just before taking lasagna from oven, sprinkle Parmesan cheese over top and return to oven for a couple minutes. This recipe can be made in a foil pan, cooled, covered tightly and frozen before baking. When ready to cook, thaw and bake as directed. Serves 12.

Carolina Bison Farm

Liver Mush Stir-Fry

1 (16-ounce) package liver mush, cut into 1-inch cubes
Vegetable oil for frying
2 cups shredded cabbage
1 onion, sliced
1 red pepper, sliced
6 green onions with tops, diced

Fry liver mush in oil until very crispy. Remove from pan and drain on paper towels. Sauté shredded cabbage, onion, pepper and green onions until tender. Top with cubed liver mush.

Chen's Restaurant 704-484-9669
Shelby's Fall Liver Mush Festival

Shelby's Fall Liver Mush Festival

3rd weekend in October

Uptown Shelby
Historic Court Square
704-487-8521
www.TourClevelandCounty.com

"Music, Mush and More" is the Shelby trademark. Although the name does it no justice, liver mush is a regional, pork-based dish that got its start mainly in central North Carolina. Curious? Visit the Official Fall Liver Mush Festival and celebrate the unique delicacy of the dish. The event features the ever-popular liver mush sandwich and liver mush pizza, stir-fry, burgers and smoked liver mush to name a few options. Can't make the festival? Liver mush is a staple in this area and can be found at most restaurants in a variety of dishes. Be sure to visit the Earl Scruggs Museum and the Don Gibson Theatre in honor of music legends who called Shelby home. Carrying on the tradition, live music is often featured on the historic court square and in local restaurants.

Bailey's Farms Shrimp and Grits

Shrimp:

1 large slice country ham
1 pound Carolina shrimp, 36 to 40 count
¾ cup scallions, cleaned and chopped thin
2 cloves garlic, minced
1 tablespoon Bailey's Farms Jalapeño Hot Sauce
1 tablespoon lime juice

Cut ham into 3 strips lengthwise, and then cut each length into ⅛-inch-wide strips. Heat a cast iron skillet over medium heat and add ham pieces. Stir well and allow ham to brown nicely. Remove ham from skillet. Add shrimp and scallions. Cook for a few minutes and add garlic. Stir in jalapeño hot sauce. Keep warm.

Cheese Grits:

2 cups quick grits
½ cup sharp Cheddar cheese, shredded
2 tablespoons butter
2 tablespoons Bailey's Farms Red Habanero Hot Sauce
Salt and pepper to taste
1 tablespoon chopped fresh cilantro

Cook according to package instructions and when they are done, stir in cheese, butter and habanero hot sauce. Season to taste with salt and pepper.

Place cheese grits in individual serving bowls and cover with shrimp-scallion mixture. Sprinkle with ham pieces and drizzle with a little lime juice and hot sauce. Garnish bowls with chopped cilantro and serve with hot biscuits.

Courtesy of Bailey's Farms, Oxford
Granville Tourism Development Authority

Starlight Café Shrimp & Grits

3 cups water, divided
1 cup grits
1 cup Gruyère
½ stick butter
Salt to taste
1 slices bacon
12 large shrimp

Flour to dust
1 cup sliced mushrooms
2 scallion, chopped
½ lemon, juiced
Pepper to taste
Tabasco to taste

Bring water to boil, add grits and simmer until soft. Add cheese, butter and salt (if grits are too thick, thin with a little water.) Heat until cheese is melted. Fry bacon in a medium sized pan over medium heat until crisp. Remove bacon and set aside. Lightly dust shrimp in flour and add to pan over medium heat. Flip shrimp once gold in color. Add mushrooms and cook until soft. Add crumbled bacon, scallion, lemon juice, salt, pepper, and Tabasco to taste. Serve over grits.

Starlight Café
Uptown Greenville

Starlight Café

*Owned and operated by
the Boutilier Family*
**252-707-9033
www.starlightcafe.org**

Located in the heart of downtown Greenville, Starlight Cafe is a family run, neighborhood restaurant in the European tradition. They feature an eclectic menu made fresh, in-house, and with local produce, meats and cheeses. The wine list is excellent and reasonably priced, and the bar serves top shelf drinks made with fresh fruits and juices. Intelligent, friendly and unhurried service makes for an enjoyable dining experience, and ongoing art exhibits complete the ambiance and of this exquisite restaurant.

Shrimp and Pea Rice Bowl

1 tablespoons extra virgin olive oil
1 pound raw shrimp, peeled and deveined
3 tablespoons shallots, finely chopped
4 garlic cloves, minced
1 cup frozen peas, cooked according to directions
1 tablespoon rice vinegar
½ teaspoon kosher salt
1 teaspoon crushed red pepper flakes
½ teaspoon ground turmeric
2 tablespoons fresh chopped parsley
4 cups brown rice, cooked

Heat oil in large skillet over medium-high heat. Add shrimp and shallots and sauté 2 minutes. Add garlic and sauté 1 minute until shrimp is done. Add peas, rice, vinegar, salt, pepper flakes and turmeric. Cook until heated through. Sprinkle with parsley and serve over rice.

Catch of the Day Cocktail Sauce

2 cups ketchup
¼ cup horseradish
Juice of 1 lemon
6 dashes Tabasco

¼ teaspoon cayenne
⅛ teaspoon Old Bay seasoning
½ teaspoon garlic salt
2 teaspoons crushed white pepper

Combine all ingredients and serve. Makes 2 cups.

From Connie's Kitchen
Shuck & Peel Party

Shuck & Peel Party

2nd weekend in November

Downtown Hickory
828-322-1121
www.downtownhickory.com

The smell of steamed oysters and fried shrimp, the taste of locally crafted beer, the sounds of Caribbean steel drums amid the ambiance of the park-like setting of Union Square are combined for a one-day party in Downtown Hickory. The Shuck & Peel Party is a mouth-watering extravaganza. The outdoor event will heighten the senses with a day of delicious food, great drink, and fun entertainment. Visit their website to learn more about Hickory's Shuck & Peel Party.

Seafood Scallop

Easy and great for company or as an accompaniment to ham.

¼ cup butter
3 tablespoons flour
1¼ cups milk
½ teaspoon paprika
Dash cayenne pepper
1 teaspoon salt
⅛ teaspoon onion seasoning
½ cup chopped mushrooms or chopped hard-boiled eggs
2½ cups cooked seafood (lobster, crab, shrimp or scallops)
½ cup buttered breadcrumbs

Preheat oven to 375°. In saucepan, melt butter. Mix in flour until smooth and then slowly add milk to make a smooth white sauce. Stir in seasonings. Add mushrooms or eggs and seafood and gently blend. Fill scallop shells or put in 1½- or 2-quart casserole dish. Top with buttered crumbs and bake 20 minutes or until crumbs are lightly browned. Serve in scallop shells or over fluffy white rice. Makes 6 servings.

Susan Moffat Thomas
MUMFEST, New Bern

Rosemary Seafood Kabobs

6 sprigs of rosemary, each about 8
    inches long
12 sea scallops
12 salmon filets, each about 2 inches
    square

12 large shrimp, shelled and deveined
1 clove garlic, minced
1 shallot, minced
2 tablespoons olive oil
Salt and pepper to taste

Remove leaves from rosemary sprigs, leaving a few on the top of each sprig. Mince the rosemary leaves.

Remove the small muscle from the scallops. In a bowl mix scallops, salmon, and shrimp with garlic, shallot, and minced rosemary. Add olive oil and salt and pepper. Marinate for 20 minutes. Thread on rosemary sprigs, alternating seafood. Cook on grill for 5 to 8 minutes.

Jean Hutchinson, Sunset Beach
Old Bridge Cookbook

Oven Fried Scallops

These scallops are very easy and fast to make. They are moist on the inside and a bit crisp on the outside.

1 egg
2 tablespoons oil
1 pound sea scallops (preferably from Bill's Seafood)
5 tablespoons seasoned breadcrumbs
Paprika

Preheat oven to 450°. Combine egg and oil, beating well with fork. Dry scallops on paper towel. Roll scallops first in the egg mixture, then lightly in the breadcrumbs. Spray non-stick baking sheet with cooking spray and arrange scallops in single layer. Sprinkle lightly with paprika. Bake 12 minutes without turning. Serve immediately.

Karen Dombrowski, Old Bridge Cookbook
Old Bridge Preservation Society

The Old Bridge Cookbook

The Old Bridge Cookbook was featured in *Our State* magazine and is a best seller. Proceeds from the cookbook help to support the restoration of the Bridge and establishment of the museum. The cookbook can be purchased at the Old Bridge or online at www.oldbridgepreservationsociety.org. Old Bridge Preservation Society is a nonprofit, 501(c)(3) organization.

Crab Cakes

1 pound lump crabmeat
1 egg, beaten
1 tablespoon chopped parsley
¼ cup finely minced shallot or green
   onion, sautéed
½ cup Ritz cracker crumbs
3 tablespoons mayonnaise

2 teaspoons yellow mustard
Juice of ½ a lemon
Salt and pepper
Dash of cayenne pepper
Flour for dredging
Old Bay seasoning for dusting

Fold ingredients together gently. Form into patties. Dredge in flour. Fry in mixture of butter and vegetable oil until browned. Lightly dust with Old Bay seasoning after crab cakes are cooked.

Graveyard of the Atlantic Museum

Graveyard of the Atlantic Museum

**59200 Museum Drive
Hatteras Village
252-986-2995 • 252-986-2996
www.graveyardoftheatlantic.com/wp/**

At the end of North Carolina Highway 12, next to the ferry terminal, the Graveyard of the Atlantic Museum attracts a lot of attention with its unique, ship-like building, porthole windows and curved timbers. One of three North Carolina Maritime Museums operated by the North Carolina Department of Cultural Resources, the museum focuses on the maritime history and shipwrecks of North Carolina's Outer Banks, often called the Graveyard of the Atlantic. Exhibitions emphasize periods from 1524 to 1945, with shipwreck artifacts and memorabilia on display and changing exhibits telling the dramatic tales of shipwrecks and life saving along the Carolina coast. The Museum holds frequent programs throughout the year. For a daily schedule of activities go to the web site and view the calendar for more information.

Crabmeat au Gratin

2 tablespoons butter
2 tablespoons all-purpose flour
1 ⅓ cups milk
1 tablespoon lemon juice
½ teaspoon salt
⅛ teaspoon white pepper

12 ounces fresh lump crabmeat
¼ cup shredded mozzarella cheese
¼ cup grated Parmesan cheese
¼ cup soft breadcrumbs
¼ teaspoon paprika
Hot cooked rice

Melt butter in a heavy saucepan over low heat; add flour, stirring until smooth, about 1 minute. Gradually add milk and then lemon juice. Raise temperature to medium and cook, stirring constantly, until smooth and thick. Stir in salt, pepper and crabmeat and blend thoroughly. Spoon seafood mixture into a lightly greased 1½-quart casserole dish and bake at 350° for 25 minutes. Combine cheeses, breadcrumbs and paprika. Sprinkle over mixture and bake an additional 3 minutes or until cheeses melt. Serve over hot rice.

Beverly Williams, Old Bridge Cookbook
Old Bridge Preservation Society

Lime Basil Grilled Trout Fillets

1 ounce fresh basil leaves
2 cloves garlic, chopped
Juice of 1 lime
¼ cup olive oil

1 teaspoon Lawry's Seasoned Salt
1 teaspoon fresh ground pepper
4 Sunburst Trout Fillets

Marinade:

Chop basil and mince garlic. Combine with lime Juice, olive oil, salt and pepper. Mix well. Add marinade to fresh trout fillets. Marinate fillets for at least 1 hour before grilling.

To Grill Trout:

Preheat well oiled grill to medium high heat. Remove fillets from marinade and place on grill flesh side down for 3 minutes. Turn to skin side down and cook 2 to 3 minutes. Serve immediately.

Sunburst Trout Farms

Sunburst Trout Farms®

**314 Industrial Park Drive
Waynesville
800-673-3051
sunbursttrout.com**

Find them on Facebook, twitter, google+, youtube and Instagram @sunbursttrout

Sunburst Trout Farms® is a 3rd generation family owned and operated trout farm growing rainbow trout below the Shining Rock National Wilderness in Haywood County. The farm offers fillets, marinated fillets, encrusted fillets, caviar, smoked trout, smoked trout dip, trout jerky, and non-trout products from the research and development kitchen; smoked tomato jam and pimento goat cheese. Trout is perfect any time of year and always in season!

Lime Basil Grilled Trout with Appalachian Ratatouille

2 teaspoons kosher salt, divided
1 cup cool water
2 small eggplant (about ½ pound), peeled and diced
4 tablespoon olive oil, divided
1 medium yellow onion, peeled and diced
6 cloves garlic, peeled and diced
1 large tomato, peeled and diced
1 teaspoon dried thyme
1 medium zucchini, seeded and diced
1 medium yellow squash, seeded and diced
1 Gala apple, cored and diced
1 Golden Delicious apple, cored and diced
1 small red bell pepper, seeded and diced
1 small green bell pepper, seeded and diced
¼ teaspoon ground cloves
¼ teaspoon ground cinnamon
⅛ teaspoon ground nutmeg
Fresh ground pepper

Combine 1 teaspoon salt with cool water. Soak eggplant in salted water for 20 minutes. Drain and pat dry on clean towels. Heat 2 tablespoons olive oil in heavy-bottom saucepan over medium heat. Add onion and garlic and cook until soft and slightly brown, 5 to 7 minutes. Add eggplant and cook 5 minutes. Add tomato and thyme and cook 8 to 11 minutes. After the tomato and eggplant mixture has cooked for 5 minutes begin cooking zucchini mixture. In a large sauté pan heat remaining olive oil over medium-high heat. Add zucchini and yellow squash; cook 2 minutes. Add apples, peppers and dry spices. Continue to cook until apples are fork tender, about 4 minutes. Combine apple mixture with eggplant mixture.

Charles Hudson
Sunburst Trout Farm

Sunburst Trout Fillet with Wilted Greens Salad and Smoked Tomato Vinaigrette

4 (6- to 8-ounce) Sunburst rainbow trout fillets
Kosher salt and fresh ground pepper to taste
¼ cup olive or vegetable oil
1 pound spinach, mustard greens or turnip greens
1 small red onion, thinly sliced
1 small yellow onion, thinly sliced
½ cup extra virgin olive oil
¼ cup cider vinegar
¼ cup Hudson's Smoked Tomato Jam

For the trout, season fillets with salt and pepper. Heat a medium to large sauté pan over medium heat. Add ¼ cup oil and heat until it dances. Add fillets flesh side down and cook about 3 minutes. Flip fish over and continue cooking another 2 to 3 minutes. Remove from pan, drain and keep warm.

For the wilted greens, thoroughly wash and dry greens. Tear or cut into ½-inch pieces Set aside in a large heat-proof bowl. Heat a medium sauté pan over medium heat. Add extra virgin olive oil and heat until it dances. Add onions and sauté until translucent. Add vinegar and jam; stir until well combined. Bring mixture to a boil and pour over greens. Toss greens and dressing with tongs. Place wilted greens on plate and top with seared trout.

Charles Hudson
Sunburst Trout Farm

Oak Planke Salmon

1 (7-ounce) salmon
Oil

Salt and pepper to taste
Fresh asparagus

Preheat convection oven. Rub salmon with oil, salt and pepper. Place on seasoned oak planke and place in convection oven for 8 to 10 minutes. Remove from oven and place on grill. Season asparagus with salt and pepper and place on grill 4 to 5 minutes. Delicious served with mashed potatoes.

Dijon Mustard Sauce:

1 tablespoon Dijon mustard
1 tablespoon heavy cream

½ tablespoon butter, softened

Combine all ingredients until well blended and serve over salmon.

Shine to Wine Festival

Lemon Caper Tuna

1 stick butter, softened
4 tablespoons capers
Juice of 2 lemons

½ teaspoon salt
½ teaspoon black pepper
4 (8-ounce) fresh tuna steaks

Combine butter, capers, lemon juice, salt and pepper to form a compound butter. Spray baking pan with nonstick spray and arrange tuna steaks so they are not touching each other. Liberally spread compound butter on top of each steak, cover with foil and bake in 375°oven 12 to 14 minutes or until cooked to your liking. Place small dollop of butter on hot tuna and serve. Makes 4 servings.

Olde Hickory Station 828-322-2356
Shuck & Peel Party

Desserts & Other Sweets

Goat Cheese Cake

6 cups water
10 ounces graham crackers
½ teaspoon ground cinnamon
½ cup unsalted butter, melted
8 ounces Buffalo Creek Farm's Plain Chèvre,
    room temperature

1 pint sour cream, room temperature
3 Buffalo Creek Farm's pastured eggs, room
    temperature
1 cup sugar
Zest and juice of 1 lemon
½ teaspoon vanilla extract

Preheat oven to 350°. In a large pan, heat water just to boiling and set aside. In food processor, combine graham crackers, cinnamon and melted butter. Process until graham crackers are finely ground and mixture holds together slightly and is evenly moistened. Wrap outside of 9-inch springform pan tightly in heavy-duty aluminum foil. Press graham cracker mixture into bottom of pan to form a ¼-inch thick crust. Smooth crust using base of juice glass. Chill, uncovered, until ready to use.

In food processor, mix chèvre, sour cream, eggs, sugar, vanilla, lemon zest and juice until mixture is smooth. Pour into prepared pan on top of crust. Place pan in center of large roasting pan and place roasting pan on center rack of oven. Pour hot water into roasting pan to a depth of 1½-inches around cheese cake.

Bake 45 minutes. Cheese cake should be firm on edges but still jiggle in center. Let cake cool in pan for at least 45 minutes at room temperature. Chill, uncovered, until ready to serve.

Buffalo Creek Farm and Creamery

Blackberry Feta Cheesecake

Crust:

1 stick butter, melted
½ cup sugar
Pinch nutmeg

2 pinches cinnamon
2 (4.8-ounce) packages graham crackers, crumbled

Mix butter, sugar and spices thoroughly. Stir into graham cracker crumbles. Coat springform pan with nonstick cooking spray and press mixture into bottom. Bake at 350° for 7 minutes. Cool completely.

Cheesecake:

3 (8-ounce) packages cream cheese, softened
1¼ cups sugar
1 cup sour cream
3 eggs

1 tablespoon vanilla extract
2 tablespoons flour
¼ cup Blackberry Pureé (recipe follows)
3½ ounces crumbled feta cheese

Mix cream cheese and sugar thoroughly. Add sour cream and mix. Add eggs and mix. Add vanilla extract and flour and mix. Add Blackberry Pureé and mix. Add feta cheese and stir thoroughly.

Blackberry Pureé:

1 cup blackberries

Sugar to taste

Blend blackberries and sugar thoroughly. Add sugar to taste. Run mixture through a fine colander or sieve to strain out seeds.

Sour Cream Topping:

1 (8-ounce) container sour cream
¼ cup sugar

1 teaspoon vanilla extract

Mix all topping ingredients thoroughly. Do not apply until sugar has completely dissolved.

After graham cracker crust has cooled, pour cheesecake into pan. Bake at 300° for 50 minutes. Do not open oven door before time is up. After 50 minutes, open oven and tap pan lightly. Only the center of the cheesecake should jiggle. Remove cheesecake and place on cooling rack. Once cooled, add Sour Cream Topping. Pipe remaining purée in a spiral on topping. Drag toothpicks through purée from the center outwards to create a spider web image. Garnish with blackberries and mint leaves if desired

Emily Miller
North Carolina Blackberry Festival

Brushy Mountain Apple Cake

4 cups flour
½ teaspoon salt
1 heaping teaspoon baking soda
2 teaspoons cinnamon
2 teaspoons allspice
2 teaspoons nutmeg
2 tablespoons ground cloves
4 eggs

2 cups sugar or honey
3 tablespoons vanilla
1½ cups cooking oil
8 to 10 cups chopped apples (these can be a variety mix or all the same)
1 cup chopped pecans or walnuts

Sift together dry ingredients. Blend eggs, sugar, vanilla and oil. Add sifted dry ingredients. Batter will be very stiff. Stir in apples and nuts. Pour into a large greased and floured tube pan and bake 1½ hours at 325° or until done. Cool on rack before removing from pan. Cover to keep moist. This cake freezes well.

Ann Jackson Garwood
Brushy Mountain Apple Festival

Fresh Apple Cake

½ cup margarine
2 cups sugar
2 eggs
2 cups all-purpose flour
1 teaspoon baking soda
1 teaspoon nutmeg

½ teaspoon cloves
½ teaspoon cinnamon
¼ teaspoon allspice
4 cups finely chopped apples
1½ cups chopped nuts

Topping:

1 cup sugar
1 stick margarine

½ cup evaporated milk
1 ½ teaspoons vanilla

Preheat oven to 325°. Cream margarine and sugar. Add eggs, 1 at a time, and beat until smooth. Sift together dry ingredients and add to egg mixture. Stir in apples and nuts. Bake in greased 9x13-inch pan for approximately 40 to 45 minutes. The egg mixture will seem dry but the apples will add some liquid as it bakes. Combine topping ingredients except for vanilla in a saucepan and cook over low heat, stirring constantly, for 10 minutes. Remove from heat and stir in vanilla. Pour over warm cake in the pan.

Apple Hill Orchard and Cider Mill

Apple-Maple Upside-Down Cake

3 tablespoons butter
½ cup maple syrup
2 medium apples
1½ cups sifted flour
2 teaspoons baking powder
¼ teaspoon salt

¼ cup shortening
¾ cup sugar, divided
2 eggs, separated
½ cup milk
½ cup grated apple

Melt butter in 9-inch round pan; add maple syrup and remove from heat. Cut cored, unpeeled apples into ½-inch slices and arrange on syrup mixture. Sift flour, baking powder and salt together. Beat shortening with ½ cup sugar and unbeaten egg yolks until fluffy. Add sifted dry ingredients and milk alternately in small amounts, beating well after each addition. Add grated apple. Beat egg whites until stiff but not dry; beat in remaining sugar and fold into batter. Spread batter evenly over apple-syrup mixture and bake at 350° for 40 to 50 minutes. Let cool 15 minutes. Place a plate on top of cake and invert cake onto plate; tap lightly to release cake. Remove pan. Serve warm with plain or whipped cream.

Brushy Mountain Ruritan Club
Brushy Mountain Apple Festival

Grammy's Dump Cake

1 (21-ounce) can blueberry or cherry pie filling
1 (16-ounce) can crushed pineapple, drained
1 stick butter, softened
1 box yellow cake mix
1 cup chopped pecans, optional

Preheat oven to 350°. Evenly spread pie filling in a 9x13-inch baking dish. Pour crushed pineapple on top and spread out as evenly as possible. In a mixing bowl blend softened butter with cake mix and stir in pecans. Spread mixture evenly on top of pineapple and bake 30 to 40 minutes until top is golden brown.

North Carolina Cotton Festival

NC Cotton Festival

1st Saturday in November

Dunn
910-892-3282
www.dunntourism.org

Over 15,000 people converge on 12 city blocks in Downtown Dunn to celebrate one of the areas prime agricultural products, cotton. Street vendors, 2 stages of entertainment, the Dunn Shriner's Car Show with over 125 unique automobiles, kiddie land, and of course a food court with delicacies to delight anyone's taste buds give the visitor a variety of choices to keep them entertained. The local cotton gin stays open and provides visitors a tour of what happens to the cotton from the field to the mill. This is a fun and educational event rolled into one!

Pineapple Cake

2 baked yellow cake layers
1 stick butter, softened
1 (3-ounce) package cream cheese,
  softened
1 (8-ounce) carton sour cream
1 cup sugar
6 ounces frozen coconut

1 (20-ounce) can crushed pineapple,
  undrained
1 small package instant vanilla
  pudding mix
1 (8-ounce) carton Cool Whip
Slivered almonds

Slice the two cake layers in half horizontally to make four layers. Set aside. Blend together butter, cream cheese, sour cream and sugar. Add coconut and pineapple. Sprinkle with dry pudding mix and stir. Fold in Cool Whip. Spread between layers and on top of cake. Sprinkle top with slivered almonds. Chill before serving.

Creedmoor Music Festival

Granville County Courthouse

Poplar Grove Plantation Cake

2 cups flour
2 cups sugar
2 teaspoons baking powder
2 beaten eggs

⅔ cup whole milk
2 teaspoons vanilla
2 sticks butter, melted

Mix ingredients together and pour into greased and floured 13x9-inch pan. Bake approximately 45 minutes at 350°. Caution opening and closing oven door to check on cake; center may fall. Serve with favorite fresh fruit.

Poplar Grove Plantation

Poplar Grove Plantation

**10200 Highway 17 North
Wilmington
910-686-9518
www.poplargrove.org**

At its height in 1860, Poplar Grove was a self-sustaining plantation, and one of the oldest peanut producing farms in the state of North Carolina. Opened as a museum in 1980, the manor house is listed on the National Register of Historic Places and sustained through the continuing efforts of Poplar Grove Foundation, Inc., a 501(c)(3) non-profit corporation dedicated to conservation, education, and preservation.

Built by Joseph Mumford Foy circa 1850, Poplar Grove Foundation, Inc. preserves the homestead of six generations of the Foy family. Open for daily tours through the manor house, the property also has craft demonstrations typical of a 19th century working community, including a blacksmith shop, weaving and basket studios as well as a Farmers' Market on Wednesdays.

Honey Bun Cake

1 box yellow cake mix
½ cup sugar
⅔ cup vegetable oil
4 eggs
1 (8-ounce) container sour cream

½ cup brown sugar
2 teaspoons cinnamon
1 cup powdered sugar
4 tablespoons milk

Mix together cake mix, sugar, oil, eggs and sour cream. Pour half into a greased and floured 9x13-inch pan. Combine brown sugar and cinnamon. Sprinkle half over batter in the pan. Add the rest of batter and top with remaining sugar mixture. Swirl sugar-cinnamon mixture back and forth with a knife. Bake at 350° for 35 minutes or until cake tests done. While cake bakes, mix together powdered sugar and milk. After removing cake from oven and while it is still warm, pour glaze over it.

The Farm at Brusharbor

The Farm at Brusharbor

**7700 Brusharbor Road
Concord
704-795-3896
www.thefarmatbrusharbor.com**

Nestled off the main road in Mount Pleasant, the Farm at Brusharbor is the perfect place to hold wedding ceremonies and receptions, family reunions, corporate events, spiritual events, social gatherings or any other reasons to get together with friends and family. The 300-acre working cattle farm is family owned and operated and provides a quintessential outdoor venue with a rustic chic appeal. The Farm is home to a perfect red barn with oversized swinging barn doors that open to beautifully lit chandlers and burlap wrapped twinkle lit décor to provide the perfect outdoor wedding with modern conveniences of an indoor barn reception. The breathtaking ceremony site overlooks one of the many ponds on the property and is a picturesque backdrop of pastures and farmland for an unforgettable setting to exchange vows.

Cinnamon Hot Cake

1 box yellow cake mix
4 eggs
⅔ cup water
¾ cup cooking oil

1 cup sour cream
1 cup brown sugar
3 teaspoons cinnamon

Mix cake mix, eggs, water, oil and sour cream. In separate bowl mix brown sugar and cinnamon. Pour half the batter into 9x13-inch pan; sprinkle half sugar mixture over batter and swirl in. Pour the rest of batter into pan and sprinkle remaining sugar on, swirling it into the batter. Bake at 325° for 40 minutes.

Glaze:

4 tablespoons milk
2 cups powdered sugar

1 teaspoon vanilla

Combine and pour over hot cake.

Creedmoor Music Festival

Hermie's Pound Cake

1½ cups corn oil
2½ cups sugar
8 eggs
1 cup self-rising flour

1 cup cake flour
1 cup cornmeal
1 teaspoon vanilla

Cream oil and sugar. Add eggs, 1 at a time, beating well after each. Add flours, cornmeal and vanilla. Bake at 325° in a greased and floured Bundt pan about 1 hour and 15 minutes, or until a cake tester inserted in the middle comes out clean.

Patricia Rhiner , 2nd Place 2008 Yates Mill Cornmeal Cook-off
Historic Yates Mill

Sour Cream Pound Cake

As seen in Cookin' up a Storm by Jane Lee Rankin of Apple Hill Farm.

1 cup unsalted butter, softened
3 cups sugar
6 eggs
3 cups all-purpose flour
¼ teaspoon baking soda
½ teaspoon salt
1 cup sour cream
1 teaspoon vanilla extract
1 teaspoon lemon extract
Powdered sugar

Grease and flour a Bundt or tube pan. Cream butter and sugar together until light and fluffy. Add eggs, 1 at a time, beating well after each addition. Sift the flour, baking soda and salt together.

Add flour and sour cream alternately to the batter starting and ending with flour. Mix only until blended. Add vanilla and lemon extracts. Pour batter into prepared pan. Bake at 325° for 1 hour and 20 minutes, or until a toothpick inserted into the center comes out clean.

Allow cake to cool in pan for 10 minutes, then run a knife around the edge and turn it out onto a rack to cool completely. Sprinkle with powdered sugar before serving.

Apple Hill Farm

White Wine Pound Cake

1 box yellow cake mix
1 (3½-ounce) box instant vanilla
    pudding
4 tablespoons white sugar
4 tablespoons brown sugar
2 teaspoons cinnamon

4 eggs
¾ cup oil
¾ cup water
½ cup Shelton Vineyards Bin 17
    Chardonnay

Combine all dry ingredients. Add remaining ingredients and mix until smooth. Bake in greased tube or bundt pan at 325° for 1 hour. Let stand 1 hour before taking out of pan.

Glaze:

½ cup white sugar
½ stick butter

¼ cup Shelton Vineyards Bin 17
    Chardonnay

Mix all ingredients. Place in saucepan and heat to a boil. Pour mixture over cooled cake.

Linda Gough
Shelton Vineyards

Favorite Chocolate Cake

2 cups flour, sifted
2 cups sugar
½ teaspoon salt
4 tablespoons cocoa powder
1 cup water
½ cup vegetable oil

1 stick real butter
2 eggs
1 teaspoon baking soda
½ cup buttermilk
1 teaspoon vanilla

Combine flour, sugar, salt and cocoa in mixing bowl. Put water, oil and butter in a saucepan and bring to a boil. Pour over dry ingredients and mix. Add eggs, baking soda, buttermilk and vanilla. Mix well and pour into greased 9x13x2-inch pan. Bake at 350° for 30 or 35 minutes until done.

Chocolate Icing:

1 stick real butter
6 tablespoons evaporated milk
4 tablespoons cocoa powder
1 teaspoon vanilla

1 (16-ounce) box 4X powdered
  sugar, sifted
1 cup chopped nuts

While cake is baking, prepare icing. Melt butter in saucepan and mix in milk, cocoa and vanilla. Remove from heat and add powdered sugar. Mix well. Stir in nuts and pour over hot cake. Let cool about 3 hours before cutting.

Touch of Heaven Alpacas

Chocolate Hershey's Syrup Cake

1 stick butter
1 cup sugar
4 eggs
1 teaspoon vanilla

Pinch salt
1 cup self-rising flour
½ teaspoon baking powder
1 cup Hershey's chocolate syrup

Cream butter, sugar and eggs; add rest of ingredients and bake in a 9x13-inch pan at 350° for 30 minutes.

Chocolate Frosting:

1 cup sugar
⅓ cup milk
1 stick margarine

½ cup semisweet chocolate chips
1 cup chopped pecans

Bring sugar, milk and margarine to a boil and boil for 1 minute. Remove from heat; add chips and stir until melted. Add nuts and pour over hot cake.

Creedmoor Music Festival

The Paca Shack at Touch of Heaven Alpacas

Granny's Kitchen Sink Cake

1 box any chocolate cake mix plus ingredients to prepare according to
    package directions
1 stick softened butter
1 small box cook-and-serve chocolate pudding
½ cup sour cream or softened cream cheese
½ (12-ounce) package mini chocolate chips

Prepare cake according to directions on box, adding ingredients
listed above. Bake in a well greased and floured tube pan according
to box directions. Frost when cool.

My Grandmama's Homemade Chocolate Icing:

½ stick butter
2 tablespoons cocoa powder
3 tablespoons milk
½ teaspoon vanilla
1 (16-ounce) box powdered sugar
Chopped nuts, optional

In small saucepan, melt butter. Add cocoa and milk and bring to
a boil, stirring constantly. Remove from heat. Add vanilla. Stir in
powdered sugar until of nice spreading consistency. Spread over
top of cake. Sprinkle with chopped nuts if desired. Enjoy!

Tracy Munn, known as "Glitter Granny"
LEAF Festival

Hummingbird Cake

3 cups flour
1 teaspoon baking soda
1 teaspoon salt
2 cups sugar
1 teaspoon ground cinnamon
3 large eggs, beaten

1 cup vegetable oil
1½ teaspoons vanilla extract
1 (8-ounce) can crushed pineapple,
    undrained
1½ cups chopped pecans, divided
2 cups chopped bananas

Cream Cheese Frosting:

Combine flour, baking soda, salt, sugar and cinnamon in a large bowl; add eggs and oil, stirring until dry ingredients are moistened (do not beat). Stir in vanilla, pineapple, 1 cup pecans, and bananas.

Pour batter into three greased and floured 9-inch round cake pans. Bake at 350° for 25 to 30 minutes or until a wooden pick inserted in center comes out clean. Cool in pans on wire racks 10 minutes; remove from pans, and cool completely on wire racks. Spread cream cheese frosting between layers and on top and sides of cake; sprinkle remaining ½ cup chopped pecans on top.

Snowbird Mountain Lodge

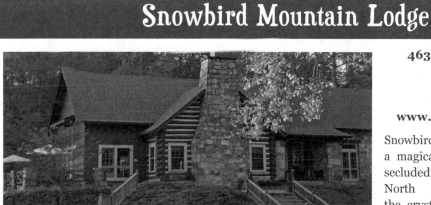

4633 Santeetlah Road
Robbinsville
828-479-3433
800-941-9290
www.snowbirdlodge.com

Snowbird Mountain Lodge is a magical, historic retreat on a secluded mountaintop in western North Carolina, overlooking the crystal-clear waters of Lake Santeetlah and the mile-high, scenic vistas of the Cherohala Skyway. Lamplight deepens the glow of the Lodge's chestnut timber. At sunrise, fingers of fog in the valleys below hold promise for a new day. The screen door claps shut softly on a breezy, warm summer evening. The sounds and scenes of Snowbird have delighted guests since 1941, healing souls and refreshing spirits with its quietly astounding smoky mountain vistas. Call or visit their website to make reservations for a relaxing and invigorating experience.

Carrot Cake

2 cups flour
2 teaspoons baking soda
3 teaspoons ground cinnamon
½ teaspoon salt
4 eggs
2 cups sugar

1 cup vegetable oil
3 teaspoons vanilla extract
2 cups shredded raw carrots
2 cups crushed pineapple, drained
1 cups shredded coconut
1 cup chopped nuts

Cream Cheese Frosting:

Preheat oven to 350°. Grease and flour 2 round cake pans; set aside. Combine flour, baking soda, cinnamon and salt. In a separate, large bowl, beat together eggs and sugar mixing until dissolved. Blend in vegetable oil and vanilla. Add carrots, pineapple, coconut and nuts. Blend well. Gradually stir in dry ingredients. Mix by hand. Pour into prepared pans and bake 25 to 30 minutes. Test with toothpick inserted in center until it comes out clean. Cool completely on wire rack. Spread cream cheese frosting between layers and on top and sides of cake.

German Chocolate Pie

1 cup sugar
2 eggs
1 (5-ounce) can evaporated milk
½ stick butter
2 tablespoon cocoa powder

¾ cup shredded coconut
¾ cup nuts
1 tablespoon vanilla
1 unbaked pie shell

Combine all ingredients except pie shell and beat well. Pour into pie shell and bake at 350° for 30 minutes.

Mrs. Geraldine Street
Creedmoor Music Festival

Chocolate Chess Pie

1½ cups sugar
5 tablespoons cocoa powder
2 tablespoons flour
¼ teaspoon salt
½ cup evaporated milk

3 large eggs, room temperature
⅓ cup unsalted butter, softened
1 teaspoon vanilla
1 (9-inch) partially baked pie crust

Preheat oven to 325°. Combine sugar, cocoa, flour, and salt. Blend in evaporated milk. Beat in eggs, 1 at a time. Add butter and vanilla, beat until smooth. Pour into partially baked pie crust. Bake 55 to 60 minutes. Cool before serving.

Imogene's Chocolate Pie

1¼ cup sugar

2 tablespoons cocoa powder

3 eggs

1 teaspoon vanilla

¼ cup milk

¼ stick butter, melted

1 unbaked pie crust

Salt

Mix sugar and cocoa. Add eggs and vanilla; beat well. Beat in milk. Add melted butter and stir to combine. Pour into pie crust. Sprinkle lightly with salt. Bake at 325° until set.

Creedmoor Music Festival

Lake Rogers

While in Southern Granville County, consider taking a peek at Lake Rogers Park; a scenic destination featuring activities for the whole family. An ideal destination spot along many road trips, Lake Rogers Park is a great place to bring children to play, to enjoy fishing, bird watching, or simply taking a break from the hustle and bustle to watch the water lap against the shore.

Lake Rogers Park
Creedmoor, North Carolina

The park boasts a 175-acre stocked lake with a fishing dock and boat ramp, paddle and jon boats available for rent during the summer season, 4 picnic shelters, parking, bathrooms, and a playground.

Tammy's Chocolate Pie

¾ cups sugar
3 tablespoons cocoa powder
3 tablespoons flour
2 cups cream

2 egg yolks, beaten
1 teaspoon vanilla
¼ stick butter, melted
1 baked pie shell

Mix sugar, cocoa and flour together; add cream and egg yolks; pour into cast iron skillet. Cook on low, stirring, until thick. Remove from heat; add vanilla and butter. Pour in pie shell and refrigerate until firm.

Creedmoor Music Festival

Creedmoor Music Festival
3rd Saturday in September

Main Street
Creedmoor

Every year, the Creedmoor Music Festival grows, both in the variety of vendors, musical groups, and in the number of attendees from near and far. There are hand-made crafts, a wide assortment of delicious foods, and live music ranging from gospel to country to classic rock. Door prizes donated by generous sponsors are awarded throughout the day, with the official Grand Prize Drawing called at noon from the center stage. Past Grand Prizes have included a weekend getaway to Myrtle Beach, and a luxury weekend getaway to Wrightsville Beach resort. Bring your family and friends and join us as we celebrate a traditional past-time the Southern way.

High Hampton Inn's Signature Black Bottom Pie

Served every Wednesday night since 1922.

Crust:

1½ cup crushed Zwieback
¼ cup powdered sugar
6 tablespoons melted butter
1 teaspoon cinnamon

Combine all ingredients; mix well. Press into pie pan, pat along sides and bottom to make crust. Bake 15 minutes at 350°.

Filling:

1 tablespoon gelatin
½ cup cold water
2 cups whole milk
4 egg yolks, lightly beaten
1¼ cup sugar, divided
4 tablespoons cornstarch
1½ cup melted chocolate

½ tablespoon vanilla
3 egg whites
1 teaspoon almond extract
¼ teaspoon salt
¼ teaspoon cream of tartar
1 cup heavy cream
2 tablespoons powdered sugar

Soak gelatin in cold water. Scald milk. Combine egg yolks, 1 cup sugar, and cornstarch, gradually stir in milk and cook over hot water in double boiler until custard forms and coats spoon. Remove 1 cup custard and add chocolate to it. Beat until well blended and cool. Add vanilla to chocolate custard and pour into pie shell; set aside. Dissolve gelatin in remaining custard, cool but do not let stiffen. Combine egg whites, almond extract, salt, and cream of tartar. Beat until stiff. Gradually add remaining sugar. Gradually fold in remaining custard and cover chocolate custard with the almond flavored custard. Chill and set. Whip heavy cream with powdered sugar and spread over top of pie. Enjoy!

High Hampton Inn

High Hampton Inn

Surrounded by the scenic Blue Ridge Mountains, historic High Hampton Inn is an Inn to remember.

1525 Highway 107 South • Cashiers
828-743-2411 • 800-334-2551 • www.HighHamptonInn.com

This captivating mountain resort is nestled on a beautiful 1400-acre private estate at 3600 feet. Guests can enjoy the renowned golf course, six clay tennis courts, fly-fishing, eight hiking trails, 35-acre private lake for swimming and boating, a world class spa, and memorable meals. Throughout each season there are special activities and events for all ages, including golf schools, a summer children's program, bridge tournaments, wildflower workshops, wellness retreats, visiting artist workshop, annual teddy bear picnic, and fun holiday weekends. High Hampton is an ideal venue for friends and families. Stay at the inn, a cottage, or a mountain rental home. Call or visit High Hampton's website for additional information or to make reservations.

Chocolate Pecan Pie

3 eggs
1 cup sugar
1 cup light corn syrup
4 ounces semi-sweet chocolate, melted
2 tablespoons butter, melted
1 teaspoon vanilla extract
1¼ cups pecans
1 (9-inch) unbaked deep-dish pie crust

Preheat oven to 350°. Combine eggs, sugar, corn syrup, chocolate, butter and vanilla in a large bowl; mix well with spoon. Stir in pecans. Pour into pie crust. Bake 50 to 55 minutes. Cool completely before serving.

Honey Pecan Pie

3 eggs
½ cup sugar
Pinch salt
½ cup dark syrup corn syrup
½ cup honey

1 stick butter, melted
1 teaspoon vanilla
1 cup chopped pecans
1 (9-inch) unbaked pastry shell

Beat eggs, add sugar and salt. Add syrup, honey, melted butter and vanilla. Stir in pecans and put into pie shell. Bake at 300° to 325° for 45 to 50 minutes.

Mary Mullinax
Kernersville Honeybee Festival

Lemon Chess Pie

2 cups sugar
4 eggs
1 tablespoon flour
1 tablespoon cornmeal
¼ cup milk

¼ cup butter, melted and cooled
¼ cup fresh lemon juice
2 tablespoons lemon zest
1 unbaked pie shell

Combine sugar and eggs and beat well. Add flour and cornmeal. Gradually add milk, butter, lemon juice and zest. Pour into pie shell. Bake in center of preheated 350° oven for 45 minutes or until set and lightly browned. Cool and chill.

Fryemont Inn

Creamy Fruit Pie

3 cups any fruit, fresh or frozen
1 deep-dish pie shell
1 cup sugar

⅓ cup flour
2 eggs
½ cup sour cream

Streusel Topping:

½ cup flour
½ cup sugar

½ stick butter or margarine

Evenly place fruit in pie shell. Mix together sugar, flour, eggs and sour cream. Pour over fruit. For topping, mix flour and sugar; cut in butter until well blended. Distribute evenly over pie. Bake at 350° for 55 to 60 minutes.

Note: For apple pie add ½ teaspoon vanilla and ¾ teaspoon cinnamon to sour cream filling. Use brown sugar instead of granulated in Streusel Topping.

Chloe Ward
Mill Spring Farm Store

Peach Custard Pie

2 eggs, beaten
1 cup sugar
2 tablespoons flour
½ cup margarine, cut into pieces

1 teaspoon vanilla
1 (9-inch) unbaked pie shell
2 cups peaches, peeled and sliced

Preheat oven to 400°. In saucepan, combine eggs, sugar and flour. Add margarine and cook on low heat until margarine melts, stirring constantly. Add vanilla. Fill pie shell with sliced peaches. Pour custard over peaches. Bake 8 minutes at 400°. Reduce oven to 350° and bake 45 minutes or until set.

Johnson's Peaches

Apple Cream Pie

¾ cup sugar
1 egg, well beaten
½ teaspoon vanilla
2 tablespoons all-purpose flour

Dash salt
1 cup sour cream
2 cups cooking apples, chopped small
1 (9-inch) deep-dish pie shell, unbaked

Topping:

3 tablespoons sugar
3 tablespoons brown sugar

⅓ cup all-purpose flour
¼ cup butter

Preheat oven to 425°. Combine the first 7 ingredients in a medium bowl until thoroughly mixed. Pour into prepared pie shell. Bake 15 minutes. Combine topping ingredients in a small bowl. Remove pie from oven and sprinkle topping mixture evenly over pie. Reduce oven temperature to 350°, and continue baking 30 to 35 minutes longer. Cool before serving. Yield: 8 servings

Bonnie Schmink
The Orchard at Altapass

The Orchard at Altapass

1025 Orchard Road
Spruce Pine
828-765-9531 or 888-765-9531
www.altapassorchard.org

Take a family hayride back in time with storytelling about "the most historically active place" along the Blue Ridge Parkway. The Orchard at Altapass, a historic apple orchard and nonprofit Appalachian cultural center, celebrates the people, music, art and natural beauty of the Blue Ridge Mountains. Over a century old, the Orchard sits astride the Parkway, preserving some of the most amazing scenery in North Carolina. Dance to live mountain music, observe craft demonstrations, hike trails, and watch bees and butterflies in the indoor observatories ... all free! Shop for heirloom apples (in season), arts and crafts, homemade fudge, and other items in the general store. Also bring the kids on Saturday mornings in summer for an Appalachian heritage experience ... a different topic every week. Be sure to come in September for Overmountain Victory Trail events. Check the website for a complete schedule. Bus parking and group tours available.

Tart n' Saucy Apple Pie

⅓ cup sugar
⅔ cup brown sugar
1 teaspoon cinnamon
½ teaspoon nutmeg
6 tablespoons flour
2 teaspoons lemon juice

2 cups canned or homemade
   applesauce
4 cups sliced tart apples
1 teaspoon grated lemon rind
Pastry for 9-inch double pie crust
3 tablespoons butter

Combine all ingredients except pie crust and butter. Mix well and pour into pie pan lined with bottom crust; dot top of filling with butter. Top with other half of pastry; seal and flute edges. Cut slits in top crust for steam to escape. Bake in 400° oven 40 to 50 minutes.

Brushy Mountain Ruritan Club
Brushy Mountain Apple Festival

Key Lime Pie

1 package unsweetened Lemon-Lime Kool-Aid
1 (14-ounce) can sweetened condensed milk
1 (8-ounce) container Cool Whip
1 graham cracker pie crust

Mix Kool-Aid and condensed milk together; fold in Cool Whip. Pour into pie crust. Refrigerate at least 1 hour before serving. The longer in refrigerator, the more the flavors blend.

Creedmoor Music Festival

Famous Muscadine Grape Hull Pie

¾ cup plus 10 tablespoons sugar
¾ cup flour
5 eggs, separated
1 quart (4 cups) grape hulls

2 tablespoons butter
1 teaspoon vanilla
2 (9-inch) baked pie shells

Mix ¾ cup sugar, flour and egg yolks together in a saucepan. Add grape hulls. Cook mixture until thickened. Stir in butter and vanilla. Pour into pie shells.

Beat egg whites until firm and then gradually beat in remaining sugar and vanilla. Divide meringue to cover the tops of each pie. Bake in preheated 350° oven 10 minutes or until golden brown on top.

North Carolina Muscadine Harvest Festival

North Carolina Muscadine Harvest Festival

Last Friday and Saturday in September

THINKSTOCK/iSTOCK/ SERGEY DORONIN

Kenansville
910-290-0525
www.muscadineharvestfestival.com

The North Carolina Muscadine Harvest Festival is the celebration of the nation's first cultivated grape and the North Carolina state fruit. The muscadine grape was first written about in 1524 when Italian explorer Giovanni Da Verrazzano discovered this grape while exploring the coast of North Carolina. This festival celebrates muscadine grape heritage and products which include vines, fresh grapes, foods, health products, and the very famous muscadine wines!! Over 20 North Carolina wineries offer tastings of over 250 different wines. Highlights include continuous beach music throughout the festival, shag dance contest, wine making contest, cooking contest, children activities, and southeastern North Carolina food favorites.

Mc Laughlin's FARMHOUSE

**15725 Mooresville Highway
Mooresville
800-985-0195 • 704-660-0971
www.mclaughlinfarmhouse.com**

*Hours of Operation:
Tuesday through Friday 8am to 5pm
Saturday 8am to 4pm*

Throughout five generations, the McLaughlin family has produced quality and fresh pork products for North Carolina. Brothers Bill and Tom, the fourth generation, decided to make these fresh pork products the signature items in their country store's inventory, but wanted to expand into other horizons. The country store offers custom made gift boxes and gift baskets, farm fresh country sausage, liver mush, sugar cured country ham, fresh hand cut western Angus beef, thick sliced smoked bacon, and home town congeniality for every visitor that walks through the door. But that's not all. There is fresh baked bread, local honey, jams and jellies, Amish cheeses, the wildly popular Hoop cheese from the NC mountains, fresh fried pies, oatmeal creme filled cookies, homemade pound cake, and old-fashioned candy. Stop by the Farmhouse, sit a spell in their gorgeous rocking chairs, and delight in deliciousness that is truly North Carolina.

Fried Fruit Pies

Filling:

6 to 7 ounces dried fruit (peaches
   or apples works great)
2 cups water
1 cup sugar

½ stick butter
1 tablespoon lemon juice
½ teaspoon ground cinnamon

Place the dried fruit in a large saucepan; add water and sugar. Bring to boil over medium-high heat, reduce to simmer and cook until fruit is tender and sugar is dissolved. Add remaining ingredients and mash together with fork. Set aside.

Dough:

2 cups flour
1 teaspoon salt
½ cup shortening

½ cup milk, plus more if needed
Vegetable oil

Combine flour and salt. Cut in shortening. Add milk and stir until soft dough forms. Divide into 10 portions. Roll each portion out on floured surface into a 6-inch circle. Place 2 tablespoons filling in each. Wet edges and fold over, sealing and crimping with a fork. In large skillet, pour oil till ¼-inch deep and heat over medium heat. Add fruit pies to hot oil and fry until browned on both sides, 3 to 4 minutes, turning as needed. Drain on paper towels.

McLaughlin's Farmhouse

Sensational Strawberry Pie

1 graham cracker pie crust
1 quart fresh strawberries, rinsed
   and hulled
3 tablespoons strawberry Jell-O
   powder

3 tablespoons cornstarch
1 cup sugar
1 cup water
Whipped cream or whipped
   topping

Fill pie shell with fresh strawberries. In saucepan, mix powdered Jell-O, cornstarch and sugar. Add water and stir. Heat over low heat until thick. Pour mixture over strawberries. Refrigerate. Serve topped with whipped cream or whipped topping.

Recipe courtesy of Buckwheat Farm
Gross Farms

Peach Cobbler

½ cup butter
1 cup flour
2 teaspoons baking powder
1½ cups sugar, divided

¾ cup milk
4 or 5 large peaches, peeled and
   sliced
½ cup water

Melt margarine in 9-inch baking dish. Mix flour, baking powder, 1 cup sugar and milk. Pour over melted margarine. Place peaches over batter. Sprinkle remaining sugar over peaches and pour water on top. Bake at 350° for 50 minutes or until golden brown.

Johnson's Peaches

Strawberry Cobbler

3 pounds frozen whole strawberries
1½ cups sugar
1 stick margarine cut into chunks
Unbaked pie crust, rolled to fit pan size

Put strawberries in 2-inch size deep baking pan. Sprinkle evenly with sugar. Dot with margarine. Cover with crust and bake at 375° for 45 minutes. Makes 4 or 5 servings.

The Historic T' Ville Diner
336-472-3322 • www.thomasvilletourism.com
Thomasville Tourism

The **T' Ville Diner** started in an old dining car purchased from Norfolk and Southern Railroad in 1936. The last meal was served in the dining car on Christmas Eve 1986. The diner has since moved to a building, but kept many of the items from the dining car including the brass light fixtures. The T' Ville Diner was the setting of the major motion picture "Above Suspicion" starring Scott Bakula and Ed Asner. The diner was named one of the top 5 diners in North Carolina by a national television food show.

Apple Cobbler

6 or 7 sweet apples (Gala, Jonagold, Golden Delicious, Cameo, etc.)
¾ cup sugar plus more for rolling apples
¾ cup quick oats
½ cup flour
5 to 6 tablespoons butter, melted
1 teaspoon vanilla

Peel, core and slice enough apples to fill your dish, about 6 for a round pie pan or a square dish depending on their size. Roll apple slices in sugar and place in dish. Mix ¾ cup sugar, oats and flour. Add melted butter and vanilla. Mix well and sprinkle on top of apples. Bake at 350° for 45 to 50 minutes or until apples are tender and top is golden. Great with or without ice cream.

J.H. Stepp Farm

J.H. Stepp Farm - Hillcrest Orchard

221 Stepp Orchard Drive
Hendersonville
828-685-9083
www.steppapples.com

In 1969, J H Stepp JR and his wife Yvonne decided to step out on faith and start the first pick-your-own farm in Henderson county. They put a sign out on the road, sat in the car and waited on people to come. They did come. They moved their whole family to Hillcrest orchard in 1967. The previous owner, Polk Hill, had allowed people to come in and pick anything left on the trees at the end of the season. The Stepp's continued to do this after they moved in. This practice and the growing stress of other businesses lead Mr. Stepp to start the pick-your-own. They started with 4 varieties selling over 50% commercially. Now they have 22 varieties and 99% pick-your-own.

The farm has grown from selling out of a car to a 10x10-foot stand to a large apple house. They also grow pick your own grapes and pumpkins and offer school tours. The farm is open from early August to around the 1st of November. Theytreat people like family and that is what sets them apart.

Blackberry Cobbler

6 cups blackberries, fresh or frozen
1½ cups sugar, divided
Zest and juice of ½ lemon
1 tablespoon cornstarch
2 cups all purpose flour
2 teaspoons baking powder
1 teaspoon baking soda
½ teaspoon salt
6 tablespoons cold butter
1 cup buttermilk
Coarse sugar for sprinkling

Grease a 9x13-inch baking dish and arrange blackberries in bottom. Stir together 1 cup sugar and lemon zest and sprinkle over berries. Blend together cornstarch and lemon juice and sprinkle over berries. Whisk together flour, baking powder, baking soda, salt and ½ cup sugar. Cut in cold butter with pastry blender until it is the texture of coarse meal. Make a well in center and add buttermilk, stirring with a fork. Crumble dough evenly over berries. Sprinkle with a little coarse sugar. Bake 40 minutes at 350° or until filling is thickened and bubbly and topping looks golden brown. Serve warm with ice cream and whipped cream.

Red Rocker Inn

NC Blackberry Festival Cobbler Recipe

There is a unique aspect to the North Carolina Blackberry Festival that allows groups and individuals in the community to make this cobbler, and there is a parade to bring them into the main square. They are arranged to create the "World's Largest Patchwork of Blackberry Cobbler." The Caldwell Chamber of Commerce provides all the ingredients except the milk and each group gets their own personalized flag to recognize their contribution. Volunteers serve over 1500 servings of free blackberry cobbler to festival goers.

1 stick butter
1 cup self-rising flour
1 cup sugar

1 cup milk
1 pint blackberries

Preheat oven to 375°. Place butter in 8x8-inch baking dish and melt in oven. In a bowl combine flour, sugar and milk. Once butter has melted pour in flour mixture. Drop berries over on top of batter. Do not stir. Then return to oven. Bake approximately 30 minutes to 1 hour, till golden brown, according to oven variations and number of cobblers being baked at one time. Makes approximately 6 servings.

North Carolina Blackberry Festival

North Carolina Blackberry Festival

July

Downtown Lenoir
828-726-0616
www.ncblackberryfestival.com

In Caldwell County, blackberries are a part of everyday life—children beg to go pick from the wild berries lining every bank and mothers take what isn't eaten during the day for cobblers. Blackberry cobblers and jam are a strong part of local heritage. The North Carolina Blackberry Festival offers summer fun to all visitors—without the chiggers! Lineberger's Killdeer Farms is on hand during the day with fresh blackberries for sale, along with other blackberry items. Arts and crafts, a variety of food vendors are available and local restaurants are open. Come join in for a BERRY good time!

Strawberry-Almond Cream Tart

Crust:

36 honey graham crackers, about 9
    sheets
2 tablespoons sugar

2 tablespoons butter, melted
4 teaspoons water

Preheat oven to 350°. Use parchment paper to line bottom of 9-inch tart pan with removable base.

Place crackers in food processor; process until crumbly. Add sugar, butter and water. Stir just until moist. Place cracker mixture in tart pan, pressing into bottom and ¾ inch up sides of pan. Bake for 10 minutes or until lightly browned. Cool on wire rack.

Filling:

⅔ cup (5 ounces) cream cheese,
    softened
¼ cup sugar

½ teaspoon vanilla extract
¼ teaspoon almond extract

Combine ingredients in medium bowl; stir until smooth. Spread mixture evenly over bottom of tart shell.

Topping:

5 cups small fresh strawberries,
    hulled, divided use
⅓ cup sugar

½ tablespoon cornstarch
1 tablespoon fresh lemon juice
2 tablespoons sliced almonds, toasted

Place 1 cup strawberries in food processor and process until smooth. Combine strawberry purée, sugar and cornstarch in small saucepan over medium heat; stir with whisk. Bring to a boil, stirring constantly. Reduce heat to low; cook 1 minute. Remove from heat. Cool to room temperature, stirring occasionally. Combine remaining 4 cups strawberries and lemon juice; toss to coat. Arrange berries in a circular pattern over filling. Spoon cooled glaze evenly over berries. Sprinkle almonds around edge. Chill 3 hours before serving. Makes 8 servings.

Kristina Harris,
1st place winner of the North Carolina 2010 Strawberry Recipe Contest
Gross Farms

Blackberry Sonker

4 cups fresh blackberries, washed
1¼ cup sugar, divided
½ cup self rising flour

1 stick butter, melted
½ cup milk
1 teaspoon vanilla

Heat berries on stove with ¼ cup sugar. Pour slightly cooked berries into square dish. In separate bowl combine 1 cup sugar, flour, butter and milk. Stir in vanilla. Pour over berries, do not stir. Cook at 350° for 30 to 40 minutes or until golden brown.

Big Elkin Creek Farm
Pat Luffman

CHRIS CASON

Big Elkin Creek Farm

197 Preacher Field Road
Elkin
336-466-4270
www.bigelkincreekfarm.com

The cabin at Big Elkin Creek Farm is a true oasis, tucked away in the foothills of North Carolina. A genuine log home built in the 1800's; it is fully furnished and has been completely updated. Located in the center of a beautiful 60-acre farm, the cabin is ideal as a couple's getaway, or perfect for families of up to six who would like to experience a taste of early pioneer days. Guests can enjoy wooded walking trails, farm animals, fishing in the pond, cozying up to the woodstove, or a simple sunrise from the rocking chairs on the front porch. Guests can choose the solitude of the farm, visit the nearby historic town and wineries, or take in the beauty of the Blue Ridge Parkway and North Carolina State Parks, just minutes away. Big Elkin Creek Farm is a memorable journey into what makes North Carolina great!

Blueberry Sonker

Sonker is a name used for a specific type of fruit cobbler from northwestern North Carolina. It is prevalent in the Mt. Airy area and Surry County. On the first Saturday in October there is a Sonker Festival held at the Edwards Franklin House in Surry County where visitors can taste different kinds of Sonker!

2 cups fresh or frozen blueberries, rinsed   **1 cup all-purpose flour**
4 fresh peaches, peeled and sliced thin   **1 egg**
1 cup sugar plus more for sprinkling   **1 stick real butter**

Mix fruit in an 8x8-inch baking dish and sprinkle 2 or 3 tablespoons sugar over it. You can add a little water, but the water left from rinsing the blueberries should be enough. Mix together flour and sugar. Add egg and mash it up with a fork until combined. It will look mealy, but really it doesn't matter too much. Dump flour mixture on top of fruit, spreading it out to cover all the fruit. Melt butter and pour on top of dry ingredients so it touches most of it. Bake at 400° until golden brown no longer than 45 to 50 minutes. Check after 40 minutes to see how fast it is baking. Serve with ice cream for a nice treat! Other flavors of Sonker to try include sweet potato, peach, cherry, apple, blackberry and strawberry.

Visit Mayberry

Peach and Blueberry Galette

1 refrigerated pie crust
1 or 2 large fresh peaches, peeled
 and sliced
1 cup fresh blueberries

3 tablespoons sugar, divided
½ tablespoon water
1 egg

Roll dough into a 13-inch circle and place on pizza stone. Mix peaches and blueberries with 2 tablespoons sugar and place in middle of dough, leaving 1 to 2 inches around edges bare. Turn edges over the fruit. Add water to egg; beat well, making an egg wash. Brush edges with egg wash. Sprinkle edges with remaining 1 tablespoon sugar.

Bake at 400° for 25 minutes or until edges turn golden; let cool to room temperature. Serve with Adagio Vineyards dessert wine, Coda.

Adagio Vineyards

Just a Peachy Cup

1 box white cake mix
1 (3-ounce) box peach gelatin
3 eggs
⅓ cup oil

1 cup water
2 tablespoons peach extract
1 to 2 cups chopped fresh peaches

Empty cake mix and peach gelatin in a bowl and stir together. In a separate bowl beat eggs, oil, water and peach extract together. Pour liquid over cake mixture and mix well. Stir in chopped peaches (amount depends on how peachy you want the cupcakes). Line cupcake tins. Scoop batter into liners. Bake at 350° for 10 to 15 minutes. Once cooled you can ice the cupcakes or eat them plain.

Katie Parsons
North Carolina Peach Festival

Johnson's Peaches

Open 7 days a week 8am to 6pm
Bus Tour please call ahead

www.johnsonspeaches.com
Candor
910-974-7730

For three generations, the Johnsons have grown quality fruit. They constantly seek newer and better varieties and use the most modern technology to produce the best peaches available. In addition to peaches, they grow nectarines, plums, apples and pears. Stop in and experience the absolute best cobbler and ice cream in the state.

Peach Dessert

First Layer:

1 cup flour
½ cup brown sugar

½ cup chopped pecans
1 stick margarine, melted

Second Layer:

1 (8-ounce) package cream cheese, softened

½ cup powdered sugar
1 (8-ounce) carton Cool Whip

Third Layer:

1 (3-ounce) box peach Jell-O
1 cup boiling water

4 to 6 cups sliced peaches.

Mix ingredients for first layer and stir to until crumbly. Spread in 13x9-inch baking pan. Bake at 350° until brown. Cool. When first layer is cool, mix ingredients for second layer and pour over first layer.

For third layer, mix Jell-O and water. Cool. Add peaches. Pour over second layer. Refrigerate until firm. To serve, top with additional Cool Whip and sprinkle with chopped nuts.

Johnson's Peaches

Apple Crisp

½ cup all-purpose flour
½ cup brown sugar
Spices to taste (cinnamon, nutmeg, allspice, etc.)
½ cup cold butter
¾ cup old-fashioned oats

½ cup slivered almonds or chopped pecans
Fuji or Honey Crisp apples
Maple syrup
Lemon juice

Preheat oven to 350°. Combine flour, sugar, spices and butter with pastry cutter or fork in medium bowl until crumbly. Incorporate oats and nuts. Fill 8 small (or 1 large) ovenproof dishes with peeled, cored and sliced apples. Drizzle with maple syrup and a few drops of lemon juice. Top with crisp mixture. Place on center rack of oven and bake until bubbly and lightly browned, approximately 30 minutes.

Haywood County Apple Harvest Festival

Granny Smith Apple Dumplings with Nutmeg Sauce

Pastry:

2 cups sifted flour
2 teaspoons baking powder
½ teaspoon salt

½ cup shortening
⅔ cup milk

Filling:

6 large Granny Smith apples, peeled
   and cored (or any tart apple)
6 (1-inch) pieces cinnamon stick

⅓ cup sugar
Butter
Milk

Sift together flour, baking powder and salt; cut in shortening. Stir in milk and mix into soft dough. Turn out and knead lightly; cut into 6 equal pieces. Roll each piece into a square large enough to hold an apple. Place 1 apple on each square. Put 1 piece cinnamon stick into center of each apple; fill remainder of cavity with sugar and butter.

Moisten edges of dough; press corners up over apples and seal; brush with milk. Bake in greased pan at 350° for 30 minutes. Serve with Nutmeg Sauce while still warm.

Nutmeg Sauce:

1 cup sugar
2 tablespoons cornstarch
2 cups boiling water

4 tablespoons butter
2 teaspoons lemon juice
2 teaspoons grated nutmeg

Mix together in saucepan sugar and cornstarch. Gradually stir in boiling water. Boil for 1 minute, stirring constantly. Stir in butter, lemon juice and nutmeg. Keep warm until time to serve.

Note: You may bake your apple dumplings in already prepared puff pastry. They will take 3 large sheets. Use half a sheet for each apple. Prepare as above and bake about 25 minutes. Prepared pastry crust may also be used.

Brushy Mountain Ruritan Club
Brushy Mountain Apple Festival

Berry Squares

Crust:

2 cups old-fashioned rolled oats
¾ cup flour
¾ cup light brown sugar
1½ teaspoon orange zest

¼ teaspoon baking soda
¼ teaspoon salt
½ cup butter, melted

Preheat oven to 350°. Combine all ingredients, mixing well. Reserve ¾ cup and press remaining mixture into 9-inch square baking dish. Bake 15 minutes.

Filling:

3 cups favorite berries
⅓ cup sugar

2 tablespoons orange juice
1 tablespoon cornstarch

Combine all ingredients, mixing well. Smooth over baked crust and crumble reserved crust mixture over top. Bake additional 25 minutes or until topping is golden brown.

The Duke Mansion

KRISTIN BYRUM PHOTOGRAPHY

The Duke Mansion

**400 Hermitage Road
Charlotte
704-714-4400
www.dukemansion.com**

Built in 1915 and tripled in size by its most famous owner James Buchanan Duke, The Duke Mansion has been home and host to leaders of the 20th century. Duke's most lasting legacies, including Duke University, Duke Energy and the Duke Endowment, took shape at this magnificent home. Listed on the National Register of Historic Places, The Mansion is operated as a nonprofit with all proceeds being used to preserve and protect this community treasure. Enjoy a stroll through its 4½ acres of gorgeous gardens and have a taste of southern hospitality while staying overnight in one of its 20 fine guest rooms. Known for its southern hospitality and cuisine, the breakfast is not to be missed.

Blondies

1½ cups flour
½ teaspoon baking powder
½ teaspoon salt
1½ cups packed light brown sugar

½ cup butter, softened
2 teaspoons vanilla
2 eggs
1½ cups chocolate chips

Preheat oven to 350°. Sift flour, baking powder and salt. Cream sugar, butter, vanilla and eggs.

Mix wet and dry ingredients until just combined. Add chocolate chips. Pour batter into well greased or parchment-lined 8x8-inch pan. Bake 15 to 20 minutes. Cut into 8 (2x4-inch) squares. Makes 8 servings.

Courtesy of Grammies Kitchen & Bakery, Creedmoor
Granville Tourism Development Authority

Caramel Brownies

2 cups sugar
¾ cup baking cocoa
1 cup oil
4 eggs
¼ cup milk
1½ cups flour
1 teaspoon salt

1 teaspoon baking powder
1 cup semisweet chocolate chips
1 cup chopped walnuts, divided
14 ounces caramels
1 (14-ounce) can sweetened
    condensed milk

Preheat oven to 350°. In a large bowl, beat together sugar, cocoa, oil, eggs and milk. In a separate bowl, combine flour, salt and baking powder; mix well. Gradually add to egg mixture; blend well. Fold in chocolate chips and ½ cup walnuts. Spoon ⅔ of batter into a greased 9x13-inch baking pan. Bake 12 minutes. While brownies are baking, combine caramels and sweetened condensed milk in a large saucepan and cook over low heat until caramels are melted, stirring constantly. Pour over baked brownie layer. Sprinkle with remaining walnuts. Drop remaining batter by teaspoonfuls over caramel layer; carefully swirl brownie batter with a knife. Bake additional 35 minutes. Do not overbake. Cool on a wire rack.

Dentzel Delight Carousel Brownies

30 Kraft (or other brand) caramels, unwrapped

⅔ cup evaporated milk, divided

½ cup unsalted butter, melted

1 (15.25-ounce) package German chocolate cake mix

¾ cup semisweet chocolate chips

½ cup chopped pecans or walnuts

Preheat oven to 350° and line bottom of 9x13-inch baking pan with parchment. Melt caramels in a small saucepan with ⅓ cup evaporated milk, stirring occasionally; set aside. Combine melted butter, cake mix, and remaining ⅓ cup evaporated milk to form dough. Press 1⅓ cups dough into pan in an even layer. Bake until puffed but not cooked through, about 7 minutes. Remove from oven and pour caramel sauce evenly over top. Sprinkle chocolate chips evenly over caramel layer.

Crumble remaining dough into bits and scatter over top. Sprinkle with chopped nuts and return to oven. Bake until brownies are puffy and set, 10 to 11 minutes more. Cool completely and cut into squares.

Burlington Dentzel Carousel

The Burlington Dentzel Carousel

336-222-5030 for additional information
Monday through Friday 8:00am - 5:00pm
www.BurlingtonNC.gov

The Burlington City Park Carousel is a 3-Row Dentzel Menagerie Carousel built around 1906-1910 at the Dentzel Carousel Company in Philadelphia, Pennsylvania. The Carousel was purchased by the City of Burlington in the summer of 1948 from Forest Park Amusement Park in Genoa, Ohio. Forest Park acquired the machine around 1924 from Locust Point Amusement Park in Oak Harbor, Ohio.

The exact date of the Carousel is not known, however, a date stamp of March and April of 1913 was found on the mirrors prior to he Carousel's restoration in 1985-87. Additionally, May 1914 was penciled on the bottom of the wooden platform. The early 1900's were known as the "Golden Era" for carousels and many were sent back to the factory for refurbishing. It is believed that the Burlington Carousel may have been built in this manner.

Chocolate Lasagna

1 package regular Oreo cookies, about 36
6 tablespoons butter, melted
1 (8-ounce) package cream cheese, softened
3¼ cups plus 2 tablespoons cold milk, divided
¼ cup sugar
1 (8-ounce) tub Cool Whip, divided
2 (3.9-ounce) packages instant chocolate pudding
1½ cups mini chocolate chips

Crush Oreo cookies into fine crumbs using a manual food processor or crush them with rolling pin or meat mallet inside a large zip-close bag.

Transfer crumbs to a large bowl. Stir in melted butter using a fork to incorporate butter into crumbs. Transfer mixture to a 9x13-inch baking dish. Press crumbs into bottom of pan. Place in refrigerator while you work on the additional layers.

Beat cream cheese with a mixer until light and fluffy. Add 2 tablespoons cold milk and sugar, and mix well. Stir in 1¼ cups Cool Whip. Spread over crust.

In a bowl, combine instant chocolate pudding with remaining milk. Whisk several minutes until pudding starts to thicken. Use a spatula to spread mixture over cream cheese layer. Allow dessert to rest about 5 minutes so pudding can firm up.

Spread with remaining Cool Whip and sprinkle mini chocolate chips evenly over top. Place in freezer for 1 hour or refrigerate 4 hours before serving.

Kathy Magcaiii
Creedmoor Music Festival

Chocolate-Covered Cherry Cookies

1½ cups all-purpose flour
½ cup unsweetened cocoa powder
¼ teaspoon baking powder
¼ teaspoon baking soda
¼ teaspoon salt
½ cup butter, softened

1 cup granulated sugar
1 egg
1½ teaspoons vanilla
2 (10-ounce) jars maraschino cherries
 (about 48) or 24 large cherries,
 halved

In large bowl, stir together flour, cocoa, baking powder, baking soda and salt; set aside.

In large bowl, beat butter with mixer on medium speed 30 seconds. Add sugar and beat on low until fluffy. Add egg and vanilla; beat well on medium speed. Gradually add flour mixture and beat on low until well blended. Shape into 1-inch balls and place 2 inches apart on ungreased cookie sheet. Press down center of each ball with thumb. Drain maraschino cherries, reserving liquid. Press 1 small or half a large cherry into center of each cookie. Bake at 350° for about 10 minutes or until done. Remove and cool on wire rack.

Frosting:

1 (6-ounce) package (1 cup)
 semisweet chocolate morsels

½ cup sweetened condensed milk

In small, heavy saucepan heat chocolate and sweetened condensed milk over low heat, stirring often until chocolate is melted. Add 4 teaspoons of reserved cherry juice. Spoon about 1 teaspoon frosting over each cookie, spreading to cover cherry. If necessary you can add more cherry juice, 1 teaspoon at a time, to thin frosting. Makes 48 cookies. Perfect with a glass of Laurel Gray Cabernet Sauvignon.

Laurel Gray Vineyards

Polynesian Coconut Pineapple White Chocolate Chip Cookies

1⅔ cups flour
¾ teaspoon baking powder
½ teaspoon baking soda
½ teaspoon salt
¾ cup butter, softened
¾ cup packed brown sugar
⅓ cup granulated sugar

1 teaspoon vanilla extract
1 large egg
2 cups white chocolate chips
1 cup flaked coconut (toasted if desired)
¾ cup mixed macadamia nuts and
   walnuts, chopped
¾ cup dried pineapple, diced

Combine flour, baking powder, baking soda and salt in a bowl; set aside. In large, separate bowl, beat butter, brown sugar, granulated sugar and vanilla extract until creamy. Beat in egg. Gradually add flour mixture. Do not over-mix. Stir in white chocolate chips, coconut and nuts along with diced pineapple. Drop by rounded tablespoon onto un-greased baking sheet. Bake at 375° for 8 to 11 minutes or until edges are lightly browned. Allow to cool slightly (up to 10 minutes) before attempting to remove.

Chefs Marti & Stormy Mongiello
© 2006 www.chefmarti.com
The Inn of the Patriots

Sarah's Peanut Butter Oatmeal Cookies

1 cup peanut butter
½ teaspoon corn syrup
½ cup sugar
½ cup brown sugar
1 teaspoon baking soda
2 eggs

1 teaspoon vanilla extract
2½ cups old-fashioned oats
½ cup semisweet or white chocolate chips
¼ cup dried cranberries, optional

Mix all ingredients together in order given. Drop by ice cream scoop onto greased cookie sheet.

Bake at 350° for 7 to 10 minutes, depending on whether you like them chewy or crispy.

1861 Farmhouse Market

The 1861 Farmhouse Market

**124 Broadstone Road
Banner Elk
828-963-6310**

The 1861 Market is an iconic landmark on the road to beautiful and historic Valle Crucis. For more than fifteen years it was known as The Ham Shoppe, and its sandwiches—served on fresh-baked bread—are legendary. Unfortunately, in 2011 The Ham Shoppe closed its doors and went out of business. Valle Crucis residents Steve and Alison Garrett decided to re-open this iconic business. They recruited many of the Ham Shoppe's former employees, who brought with them the wonderful recipes that had made the little sandwich shop and bakery famous. Today, customers still enjoy not only "The World's Best Sandwiches"—many of them featuring mouth-watering, honey-glazed ham—but also delicious home-made sides like Southern Potato Salad, Cole Slaw, Farmhouse Chili, and a variety of scrumptious desserts.

The Market proudly showcases many products from local craftsmen, including pottery, birdhouses, walking sticks, and jewelry—along with unique vintage finds—making The 1861 Farmhouse Market a great place to pick up a special gift or a memento of your trip to the mountains.

Yates Mill Cornmeal Pecan Sandies

½ cup butter
1 cup sugar
1 large egg
1 teaspoon vanilla extract
½ cup chopped pecans
1 cup all-purpose flour
½ cup Yates Mill white cornmeal
1 teaspoon. baking powder
½ teaspoon salt

Preheat oven to 350°. Cream butter and sugar together, add egg and vanilla and stir until well blended. Sift cornmeal, flour, baking powder and salt together in a separate bowl. Add dry ingredients to wet and mix until a dough forms. Mix in pecans until well distributed throughout dough. Shape dough into balls about 1 inch in diameter, and then flatten slightly on an ungreased cookie sheet. Bake 9 to 11 minutes, until edges are just browned. Cool cookies on sheet for a couple of minutes before removing them to a rack to cool completely.

Jeanne Robbins,
3rd Place 2007 Yates Mill Cornmeal Cook-off
Historic Yates Mill

Grammy's Delicious Molasses Cookies

¾ cup butter, softened
1 cup sugar plus more for rolling
   cookies
¼ cup molasses
1 egg
2 teaspoons baking soda

2 cups flour
½ teaspoon cloves
½ teaspoon ginger
½ teaspoon salt
1 teaspoon cinnamon

Mix butter, 1 cup sugar, molasses and egg. In separate bowl, mix baking soda, flour, cloves, ginger, salt and cinnamon. Combine moist and dry ingredients and chill for 4 hours. Using a spoon, form ¼-inch dough balls and roll in sugar. Place on greased cookie sheet and bake at 400° until brown on top. Bake a minute or two longer for crisper cookies.

Margaret R. Varn
Catawba Science Center

Chocolate No-Bake Cookies

2 cups sugar
½ cup milk
1 stick butter
¼ cup cocoa

1 pinch salt
1 teaspoon vanilla
½ cup peanut butter
2½ cups old-fashioned oats

Combine sugar, milk, butter, cocoa and salt in a medium saucepan; cook over medium heat until mixture comes to a boil. Boil while stirring for approximately 4 to 5 minutes until a drop forms soft-ball stage (234° to 240° on candy thermometer). Remove from heat and stir in vanilla, peanut butter and oats. Spoon small amounts onto wax paper and let cool.

Creedmoor Music Festival

Cookie Delight

1 package Chips Ahoy chocolate chip cookies
2 cups milk
1 or 2 (8-ounce) cartons Cool Whip, thawed
1 jar Hershey's chocolate fudge, room temperature

Dip cookies individually in milk and line the bottom of 9x13-inch glass baking dish. Be sure not to soak cookies too much as you want them to be slightly crunchy. Gently fold 1 layer of Cool Whip on top of cookies. Spoon dollops of chocolate fudge onto Cool Whip. Add another layer of cookies and finish with a layer of Cool Whip. Top dessert with crumbled chocolate chip cookies. Chill and serve.

Neuse River Music Fest

My Grandma's Ladyfinger Recipe

1½ cups sugar
6 sticks softened Land O' Lakes salted butter (this is the secret)
6 teaspoons vanilla
6 cups plain flour, sifted
1½ teaspoons salt
3 cups chopped pecans

Cream sugar and butter together. Add other ingredients. Roll into finger-shaped cookies. Bake at 350° for 20 minutes. Makes about 16 dozen.

Mary M. Rose, Planning Director
Christmas in the City

Old Fashion Blueberry Bread Pudding

4 cups bread cubes
1 cup blueberries
1 apple, cored, peeled and chopped
4 cups milk
6 tablespoons butter

1 cup sugar
4 eggs
1 teaspoon salt
1 teaspoon vanilla
1 teaspoon cinnamon

Preheat oven to 350°. Mix bread cubes with blueberries and apple and put into a 2-quart buttered baking dish. Scald milk with butter and sugar. Lightly beat eggs and salt and stir in warm milk mixture. Add cinnamon and vanilla. Pour over bread and fruit. Set baking dish into a larger dish. Add enough water to larger dish to reach up to level of pudding. You do not want water to boil over into pudding. Bake at 350° for 1 hour.

Ann Debnam
North Carolina Blueberry Festival

Our Favorite Banana Pudding

2 small boxes banana cream flavor Jell-O instant pudding
3 cups milk
1 (14-ounce) can sweetened condensed milk
2 (8-ounce) cartons frozen whipped topping
1 box vanilla wafers
3 to 4 bananas, sliced

Mix pudding mix and 3 cups milk until creamy. Add condensed milk and 1 carton whipped topping. Mix until creamy. In 9x13-inch baking dish, layer wafers, bananas and pudding 2 times, top with remaining whipped topping. Can top with a few crushed wafers if desired. Refrigerate until ready to eat.

Sonya Snyder, Town of Cary Parks,
Recreation and Cultural Resource Department
Cary Kite Festival

Lazy O Farm

Just Peachy Pudding

1 (8-ounce) package cream cheese, room temperature
1 (14-ounce) can sweetened condensed milk, divided
1 (8-ounce) container sour cream
3 tablespoons peach extract, divided
1 (3-ounce) box peach gelatin
2 (3-ounce) boxes vanilla pudding
1 cup milk
⅓ cup whipping cream
1 (16-ounce) tub Cool Whip
1 box vanilla wafers
3 to 4 peaches, peeled and sliced

Place cream cheese, one quarter of the sweetened condensed milk, sour cream and 1 tablespoon peach extract into a bowl. Mix with mixer until smooth. Mix peach gelatin and vanilla pudding together in a bowl. Add the remaining sweetened condensed milk, 1 cup milk and whipping cream. Beat with mixer until smooth. Add rest of peach extract and mix until smooth. Combine with sour cream mixture and mix until blended smoothly together. Add Cool Whip and mix until smooth.Spread half the vanilla wafers in a deep-dish pan. Layer half the sliced peaches on top of wafers. Spread half the pudding mixture on top of peaches. Repeat layers 1 more time. You can decorate the top with additional Cool Whip or more peaches if desired. Chill before serving.

Lisa Roland,
1st Place, Adult Peach Dessert Cooking Contest
North Carolina Peach Festival

Cherry Divine

1 tablespoon butter
½ cup flour
⅔ cup sugar
¼ cup milk

3 large eggs
2 teaspoons vanilla extract
Dash of salt
12 ounces pitted fresh cherries

Preheat oven to 350°. Combine butter, flour, sugar, milk, eggs, vanilla and salt; whisk well, forming thin batter. Place cherries into greased 2-quart baking dish. Pour over cherries and bake 45 minutes, or until cherry custard is browned and puffed around the edges, and the center is set. Cool slightly before serving.

Mount Mitchell Crafts Fair

1st Friday and Saturday in August

Town Square • Burnsville
828-682-7413

With approximately 200 juried crafts, the annual Mount Mitchell Crafts Fair more than qualifies as a craft shopper's paradise, as evidenced by the over 25,000 people who attend this event each year, searching for those special, one-of-a-kind items created by artisans from across the Blue Ridge. Shoppers browse a wide selection of items, including handmade quilts, jewelry, hand-turned wooden household items, various types of pottery, art fabrics, rustic furniture, traditional mountain musical instruments, blacksmith creations, candles, soaps, lotions, and artwork of all mediums. Have a seat and watch as the artisans produce their craft throughout the day. Enjoy a lunch of southern favorites such as barbeque and sweet tea on the square and listen to live music and entertainment, or perhaps try to keep up with the cloggers and other dancers as they kick up their heels on stage. Step back into the past and enjoy an old-fashioned Town Square event that exhibits Southern Hospitality at its best. Burnsville is located in Yancey County, home of Mount Mitchell, the highest peak east of the Mississippi at an elevation of 6,684 feet. Burnsville is 20 miles from the Blue Ridge Parkway and 35 miles northeast of Asheville.

Rice Supreme

½ cup rice
1½ quarts (6 cups) boiling water
1 quart milk, divided
¾ cup sugar, divided
1 teaspoon salt

1 tablespoon butter
3 envelopes unflavored gelatin
½ cup cold water
1 pint heavy cream
2 tablespoons vanilla

Pour rice into boiling water and boil briskly for 2 minutes. Drain and rinse in cold water and return to pan. Add 2 cups milk, 1 tablespoon sugar and salt. Bring to boil and add butter. Cover and simmer 20 minutes. Do not stir. Pour into bowl, add remaining milk and sugar and let cool. Soften gelatin in cold water 5 minutes and heat slowly until gelatin dissolves. Add to rice. Chill until thick enough that rice grains won't sink. Whip cream and add vanilla. Fold into rice and pour into mold or 8x11-inch pan and chill overnight. Serve with Cherry Sauce. Makes 8 servings.

Cherry Sauce:

3 cups sour cherries, pitted
1 cup water
1 tablespoon lemon juice
⅔ cup sugar

2 tablespoons cornstarch
¼ cup water
1 tablespoon butter, optional
Red food coloring, optional

Bring cherries, water, lemon juice and sugar to a boil. Mix cornstarch with water and stir into sauce. Cook, stirring, until thick and clear, 2 or 3 minutes. Remove from heat; add butter and a few drops red food coloring if desired. Chill before serving.

Susan Moffat Thomas
MUMFEST, New Bern

Local Berry Good Popsicles

1 cup yogurt
3 to 4 teaspoons honey
1 cup local blueberries or blackberries
1 to 2 tablespoons lemon juice
2 ripe bananas

Using a blender, puree yogurt, honey, berries, and lemon juice. Add bananas and puree well. Spoon mixture into popsicle molds or 8 to 10 small paper cups. If using cups, place foil over top of each cup and pierce center of foil and insert a wooden popsicle stick. Place in freezer 5 to 6 hours or until hard frozen. Before serving, dip cups or molds in warm water for a few seconds to release popsicle from mold or cup.

Appalachian Sustainable Agriculture Project

Homemade Blueberry Ice Cream

This one is a favorite of the vendors and patrons at the Columbus County Community Farmers Market. I make it with fresh blueberries, but you can easily substitute peaches, strawberries, or any other fresh fruit.

4 cups fruit
1 cup sugar
1 (12-ounce) can evaporated milk
1 (3¾-ounce) package vanilla instant pudding mix
1 (14-ounce) can sweetened condensed milk
4 cups half-and-half

Combine fresh fruit and sugar; let stand 1 hour. Process in food processor until smooth, stopping to scrape down sides. Stir together evaporated milk and pudding mix in a large bowl; stir in fruit purée, condensed milk and half-and-half. Pour mixture into freezer container of a 4-quart hand-turned or electric freezer; freeze according to manufacturer's instructions. Spoon into an airtight container and freeze until firm. Makes 2 quarts.

Myra Tyner Godwin
Columbus County Community Farmers Market

Butter Mint Pats

Passed down from Catherine Graham McElroy, Billy Graham's sister. It's a favorite of all of the Graham women.

1 cup butter, softened
1 cup butter mints, crushed

2 cups all-purpose flour
1 tablespoon sugar

Cream butter at medium speed in large mixer bowl until light; add crushed mints. Add flour, blend well at low speed. If necessary, chill dough for easier handling. On wax paper, roll out or pat dough into a 9-inch square. Sprinkle with sugar. Cut into 1¼-inch squares using tiny cutters. Place on ungreased cookie sheets. Bake at 300° for 18 to 20 minutes until pale golden brown. Do not over bake. Makes 36.

Billy Graham Library

The Billy Graham Library

4330 Westmont Drive
Charlotte, NC 28217
704-401-3200
BillyGrahamLibrary.org

Admission Is Free.
The Experience Is Priceless.

More than 100,000 visitors each year explore the historical re-creations and state-of-the-art exhibits at the Billy Graham Library in Charlotte. They have the opportunity to tour Billy Graham's boyhood home and the main 40,000-square-foot facility, which houses six exhibits, four galleries of memorabilia from around the world, and two theaters covering the span of Graham's lifetime ministry. Guests can also stroll through the prayer garden, relax over lunch in the Library's café, and buy unique gifts in its bookstore.

Christmas at the Library, which runs most of the month of December, is a special celebration for the entire family that focuses on the true meaning of Christmas—the birth of Jesus Christ—and features a live nativity, horse-drawn carriage rides, carolers, sparkling lights, storytelling for children, holiday treats, and more.

Just Peachy Fudge

1 fresh peach
3 cups sugar
⅔ cup heavy cream
1½ sticks butter
1 (7-ounce) jar marshmallow crème
1 (12-ounce) package white chocolate chips
3 teaspoons peach extract
12 drops yellow food coloring
9 drops red food coloring

Grease 9x13-inch pan. Chop peach. In saucepan over medium heat, combine sugar, heavy cream and butter. Heat to softball stage (234° to 240° on candy thermometer). Remove from heat and stir in marshmallow crème and white chocolate chips. Mix well until chips are melted and mixture is smooth. Remove 1 cup and set aside. To the remaining mixture add the flavoring, food colorings and chopped fresh peaches. Stir well and pour into prepared pan. Pour reserved mixture over top and swirl layers for a decorative look. Chill 2 hours until firm. Cut into small squares and store in an airtight container in freezer.

North Carolina Peach Festival

Index

North Carolina State Flower:
Cornus florida

Index of Events & Destinations

This Index is meant to be a tool for locating all events and destinations featured in *Eat & Explore North Carolina*. Each event or destination is listed by both name and city referencing the page number for its featured page. Events and destinations that have a recipe are additionally listed by event or destination name then recipe, referencing the page number for the recipe. A complete Index of Recipes begins on page 255.

Index of Recipes

North Carolina Blackberry Festival

Brushy Mountain Apple Festival

Apple Hill Farmv

Carolina Bison Farm

About the Author:

In 1999, Christy Campbell began her journey in the world of cookbooks when she took a position at a publishing company specializing in regional cookbooks. At the time, it was an all-new experience, so she immersed herself in cookbooks, both at home and at the office. With the help of the associate publisher and her personal mentor, Sheila Simmons (author, STATE HOMETOWN COOKBOOK SERIES), Christy learned the in's and out's of the small press world, devoting herself to cookbooks for the next 6 years. After the birth of her youngest son, Campbell took a sabbatical from the publishing world to focus on her young family.

In 2009, Campbell reconnected with Sheila Simmons and began work with Great American Publishers, reenergizing a 10 year love of cookbooks. She is now an integral part of Great American Publishers and has begun a new cookbook series of her own. The EAT & EXPLORE STATE COOKBOOK SERIES chronicles the favorite recipes of local cooks across the United States while highlighting the most popular events and destinations in each state.

When she is not writing cookbooks, selling cookbooks or cooking recipes for cookbooks, Christy Campbell enjoys volunteering at her children's school, running and reading. She lives in Brandon, Mississippi, with her husband Michael and their two sons.

State Hometown Cookbook Series
A Hometown Taste of America, One State at a Time

EACH: $18.95 • 240 to 272 pages • 8x9 • paperbound

The STATE HOMETOWN COOKBOOK SERIES captures each state's hometown charm by combining great-tasting local recipes from real hometown cooks with interesting stories and photos from festivals all over the state. As a souvenir, gift, or collector's item, this unique series is sure to take you back to your hometown... or take you on a journey to explore other hometowns across the country.

Georgia Hometown Cookbook • 978-1-934817-01-8

Louisiana Hometown Cookbook • 978-1-934817-07-0

Mississippi Hometown Cookbook • 978-1-934817-08-7

South Carolina Hometown Cookbook • 978-1-934817-10-0

Tennessee Hometown Cookbook • 978-0-9779053-2-4

Texas Hometown Cookbook • 978-1-934817-04-9

- Easy to follow recipes produce great-tasting dishes every time.
- Recipes use ingredients you probably already have in your pantry.
- Fun-to-read sidebars feature food-related festivals across the state.
- The perfect gift for anyone who loves to cook.
- Makes a great souvenir.

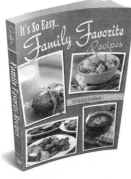

Family Favorite Recipes

It's so easy to cook great food your family will love with 350 simply delicious recipes for easy-to-afford, easy-to-prepare dinners. From **Great Grandmother's Coconut Pie**, to **Granny's Vanilla Wafer Cake,** to **Mama's Red Beans & Rice**, this outstanding cookbook is the result of decades of cooking and collecting recipes. It's so easy to encourage your family to eat more meals at home...to enjoy time spent in the kitchen... to save money making delicious affordable meals...to cook the foods your family loves without the fuss...with *Family Favorite Recipes*.

$18.95 • 248 pages • 7x10 • paperbound • 978-1-934817-14-8

www.GreatAmericanPublishers.com • www.facebook.com/GreatAmericanPublishers

Eat & Explore Cookbook Series

EAT AND EXPLORE STATE COOKBOOK SERIES is a favorite of local cooks, armchair travelers and cookbook collectors across the United States. Call us toll-free 1.888.854.5954 to order additional copies or to join our Cookbook Club.

EACH: **$18.95 • 240 to 272 pages • 7x9 • paperbound**

Arkansas	Minnesota	North Carolina	Oklahoma	Virginia	Washington
978-1-934817-09-4	978-1-934817-15-5	978-1-934817-18-6	978-1-934817-11-7	978-1-934817-12-4	978-1-934817-16-2

Don't miss out on our upcoming titles—join our Cookbook Club and you'll be notified of each new edition.

www.GreatAmericanPublishers.com • www.facebook.com/GreatAmericanPublishers

ORDER FORM

Mail to: Great American Publishers • P. O. Box 1305 • Kosciusko, MS 39090

Or call us toll-free 1.888.854.5954 to order by check or credit card

❏ Check Enclosed
Charge to: ❏ Visa ❏ MC ❏ AmEx ❏ Disc

Card # _____

Exp Date Signature _____

Name _____

Address _____

City/State _____

Zip _____

Phone _____

Email _____

Qty.	Title	Total
____	_____	____
____	_____	____
____	_____	____
____	_____	____
____	_____	____
____	_____	____
	Subtotal	____
	Postage ($3 first book; $0.50 each additional)	____
	Total	____